SCOTTISH LIGHTHOUSE PIONEERS

SCOTTISH LIGHTHOUSE PIONEERS

TRAVELS WITH THE STEVENSONS IN ORKNEY AND SHETLAND

PAUL A. LYNN

Whittles Publishing

Published by
Whittles Publishing Ltd.,
Dunbeath,
Caithness, KW6 6EG,
Scotland, UK

www.whittlespublishing.com

© 2017 Paul A. Lynn

ISBN 978-184995-265-1

Printed by Melita Press, Malta.

CONTENTS

PREFACE

The Stevenson engineers pioneered a marvellous set of lighthouses around the coasts of Scotland in the 19th century – lighthouses which inspire today's visitors with their architectural elegance, and speak of compassion for sailors and fishermen risking their lives in notoriously dangerous waters.

Much has been written in recent years about the Edinburgh-based Stevenson family and their engineering achievements. Yet for many of us there remains something of a mystery. What was it actually like to be a Scottish lighthouse engineer, and how did his professional activities interact with social and economic conditions in Scotland at the time? How did the Northern Lighthouse Board's Engineer (almost invariably a Stevenson) cope with weeks aboard a small lighthouse vessel, traveling around the Scottish coast on tours of inspection and interacting with highlanders and islanders in some of the remotest regions of Europe?

Fortunately two of Scotland's most celebrated literary sons witnessed Stevenson lighthouse engineering at first hand, and left us fascinating, but little known, accounts of their experiences. Sir Walter Scott was a famous poet and member of the Edinburgh establishment; Robert Louis Stevenson was a family member and troubled engineering apprentice desperate to become an author. Much of this book is devoted to their reminiscences.

The first two chapters set the scene, with a journey to the Orkney and Shetland Islands and descriptions of the chain of Stevenson lighthouses that illuminate a vital shipping route between the North Sea, Baltic, and North Atlantic. Chapter 3 introduces the remarkable Stevensons – principally Robert, founder of the dynasty, and his sons Alan, David and Thomas. Chapters 4 and 5 give the stage to Sir Walter Scott and Robert Louis Stevenson, son of Thomas. And finally we travel to Muckle Flugga, northernmost outpost of the British Isles and last link in the chain, a vicious rock on which Thomas and David Stevenson dared to build their 'impossible lighthouse'.

I hope this book will open up new horizons to lighthouse enthusiasts, and encourage visitors to the Orkney and Shetland Islands to explore their remarkable lighthouse heritage.

Paul A. Lynn

Acknowledgements and references

I am very grateful to the following copyright owners for permission to include images which do so much to bring this story to life:

Northern Lighthouse Board (NLB), Edinburgh
National Library of Scotland (NLS), Edinburgh
Ian Cowe
Roland Paxton
Tommy Hyndman
Paul Warrener

and the following Geograph contributors:

James Allan	Julian Paren	Andy Strangeway
Oliver Dixon	Mike Pennington	Andrew Tryon
Rob Farrow	M.J. Richardson	Colin Wheatley
Liz Gray	Dorcas Sinclair	Stuart Wilding
Christopher Hilton		

All the above are individually acknowledged in the text, as are a number of Wikipedia images.

Other photographs and images are my own, or are reproduced from historical works that are out of copyright. Two images of the Bell Rock lighthouse have been obtained from Robert Stevenson's 1824 Account, digitised by the Internet Archive in 2012 with funding from the Northern Lighthouse Heritage Trust. The Northern Lighthouses insignia and an image of the Eddystone, Bell Rock, and Skerryvore Lighthouses are photographed from my copy of Alan Stevenson's 1848 Account.

I have referred to various books and websites while writing this book. I make no claims for originality in the historical material on lighthouses or the Stevenson family, and am grateful for the efforts of those who have researched these topics before me. I would particularly like to mention *The Lighthouse Stevensons* by Bella Bathurst; *Dynasty of Engineers* by Professor Roland Paxton; *The Letters of Robert Louis Stevenson* (Yale University Press, Booth and Mehew, eds.); and the websites of the Northern Lighthouse Board (www.nlb.org.uk) and the Bell Rock Lighthouse (www.bellrock.org.uk).

1 FROM JOHN O' GROATS TO MUCKLE FLUGGA

A signpost at the northeast tip of the Scottish mainland advertises one of the best-known distances in the English-speaking world: 874 miles to Land's End, the southwest tip of England. A magnet for dedicated cyclists and super-fit runners, 'Land's End to John o' Groats' – or the other way round – is widely regarded as a suitable endurance test for generating donations to charity, or proving something to somebody. Its fame is so great that separate records exist for completion by motorcycle, skateboard, and wheelchair.

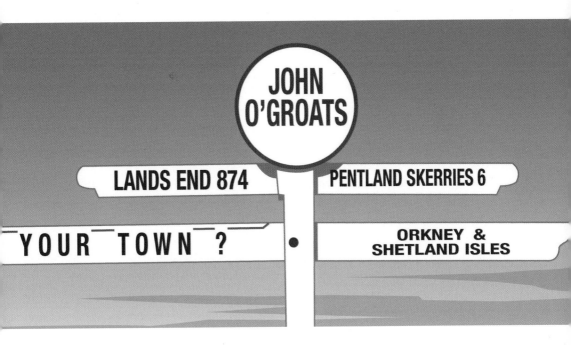

In precisely the opposite direction, the signpost announces a modest 6 miles to the Pentland Skerries, a group of four rocky islets. Modest, that is, until we realise that they are set in one of the most vigorous stretches of tidal water in the world. The Pentland Firth, which separates the Orkney Islands from the north coast of Scotland, has long

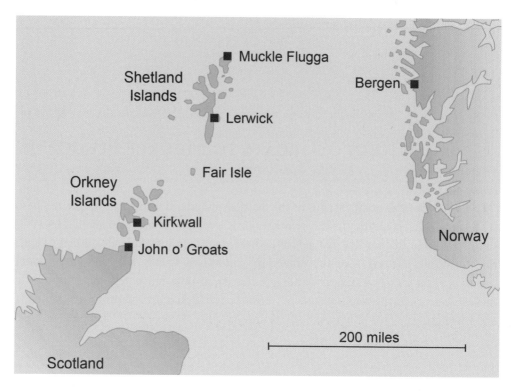

The Orkney and Shetland Islands, collectively known as the Northern Isles.

been a hazard for the inexperienced mariner and is nowadays recognised as a potential powerhouse of marine energy. Although it cannot tempt cyclists or runners, a super-fit swimmer managed to cross it in 2011. 'Hell's Mouth', the eastern entrance to the firth, is guarded by the historic Pentland Skerries Lighthouse.

The signpost also advertises Orkney and Shetland, collectively known as the Northern Isles, but is shy about distances. Orkney, with capital Kirkwall and a total population of around 20,000, is actually quite close – an archipelago of 70 scattered islands, 17 of them inhabited, that starts just across the Pentland Firth and continues northwards for 50 miles. Shetland, with capital Lerwick and a similar population, is almost another world. Maps of Britain and Scotland generally put it in a box of its own, obscuring the wild expanse of ocean that divides it from Orkney. The razor rock of Muckle Flugga at its far northern tip is about 200 miles from John o' Groats on a latitude similar to Bergen; perched on top is another historic lighthouse, surely one of the most dramatically situated in the world.

A journey along the wild eastern coastlines of Orkney and Shetland has special attractions for the lighthouse enthusiast. There are 11 classic lighthouses in all, including two on Fair Isle. They were built between 1789 and 1915 by a remarkable group of engineers who devoted much of their lives to lighting the coasts of Scotland. First in line was Thomas Smith, appointed Engineer to the newly-formed Northern Lighthouse Board in 1787. He was followed by Robert Stevenson in 1807 and, in turn, by Robert's sons Alan, David, and

Thomas, and two grandsons, David Alan and Charles. The Stevenson dynasty of engineers became virtually synonymous with Scottish lighthouse engineering in the 19th and early 20th centuries.

Fortunately two of Scotland's most famous literary sons left fascinating eye-witness accounts of the Stevenson engineers. The first, Sir Walter Scott (1771–1832), poet and author of the *Waverley* novels, had a deep love of the Highlands and Islands; the second, Robert Louis Stevenson (1850–94), was a family member who abandoned an unhappy engineering apprenticeship to become a world-famous storyteller. Both experienced life aboard the Northern Lighthouse Board's yacht on 19th-century voyages of inspection around the Scottish coast, including Orkney and Shetland, and wrote memorably about the Stevensons' professional lives, personalities, and the socioeconomic context in which they worked. We will open this treasure chest a little later; but first we set the scene with some historical notes on the magical Northern Isles, and descriptions of the classic lighthouses along their eastern coastlines.

2 The Northern Isles and their lighthouses

Orkney

The Orkney Islands boast one of the most impressive collections of prehistoric sites in Europe. A Stone Age culture developed and flourished as early bands of hunter-gatherers were joined by farmers moving across the Pentland Firth to settle in the fertile islands. Local sandstone, often available on the shore as convenient building slabs, has left standing stones, chambered tombs and buildings, including the oldest remaining stone house (3500–3100 BC) yet discovered in northern Europe, which comfortably predates the pyramids of Egypt. The internationally famous settlement of Skara Brae (2200–1700BC) includes a number of dwellings linked by low passageways and gives startling evidence of a well-ordered domestic life. Many of Orkney's monuments, including the Standing Stones of Stenness, speak of the elaborate rituals of a people living far from Europe's traditional centres of civilisation.

The Stone Age settlement of Skara Brae, Orkney (Geograph/Christopher Hilton).

Standing Stones of Stenness, Orkney (Geograph/Andrew Tryon).

During the early Iron Age (800–500BC) Orkney's climate became colder and wetter, forcing farmers onto the more fertile low-lying areas. Impressive stone brochs, or round towers, began to appear, probably for defence. The Romans were aware of the islands and traded with their inhabitants, but failed to occupy. By the 7th century AD the local tribes had fused with the Picts ('painted people') of northern Scotland, and Celtic missionaries were making contact. But early Christianity suffered a severe setback with the arrival of pagan Viking hordes who, in the early 9th century, chose Orkney as a centre for their raids. It remains unclear whether they obliterated or merely tolerated the Picts, but one fact is certain: Orkney's way of life soon became essentially Norse.

Norwegian rule proper began in AD875 and lasted for 600 years. The Orkney Islands were finally returned to Scotland in 1472 following a pledge by the King of Norway to the King of Scotland as part of a marriage contract. Orkney's history coalesced with that of mainland Scotland and, eventually, Great Britain. But today's visitors are often surprised by the evidence and extent of Norse influence.

In modern times Orkney is perhaps most famous for Scapa Flow, a huge deep-water anchorage encircled and protected by a cluster of islands. The Royal Navy used it as a base in World War I to prevent German warships reaching the North Atlantic. After the 1918 Armistice the German fleet was transferred to Scapa Flow to await its

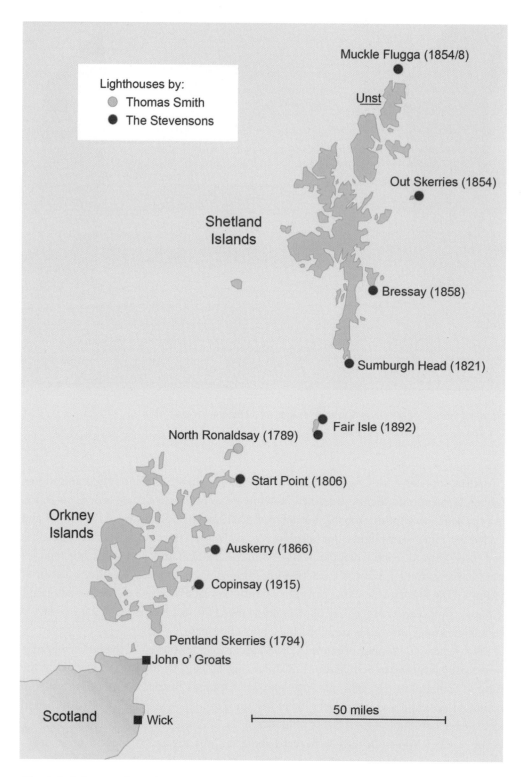

Legend:
Lighthouses by:
- Thomas Smith
- The Stevensons

Muckle Flugga (1854/8)

Unst

Out Skerries (1854)

Shetland Islands

Bressay (1858)

Sumburgh Head (1821)

Fair Isle (1892)

North Ronaldsay (1789)

Start Point (1806)

Orkney Islands

Auskerry (1866)

Copinsay (1915)

Pentland Skerries (1794)

John o' Groats

Scotland

Wick

50 miles

Classic lighthouses along the eastern coastlines of Orkney and Shetland.

fate, but the sailors opened the seacocks and sent their ships to the bottom. Most were subsequently salvaged, but remaining wrecks still attract curious divers. Scapa Flow hit the headlines again at the start of World War II, when the battleship HMS *Royal Oak* was sunk by a German U-boat with the loss of more than 800 men. The disaster proved that a submarine could thread its way between the encircling islands and led to the construction of causeways known as 'Churchill Barriers'. As a result you can now do some of your island-hopping by land.

Our travels with the Stevensons begin as we cast off from the small harbour at John o' Groats and seek out the five classic lighthouses that guide sailors along Orkney's eastern coastline.

PENTLAND SKERRIES LIGHTHOUSE

Engineer: Thomas Smith   Year established: 1794
Location: Muckle Skerry, the largest of the four Pentland
Skerries, at the eastern end of the Pentland Firth
Latitude: 58° 41.4' N   Longitude: 2°55.5' W
Nominal range: 23 nautical miles   Elevation: 170 feet (52 metres)
Character: Flashing (3) white every 30 seconds   Automated: 1994

Pentland Skerries Lighthouse (NLB).

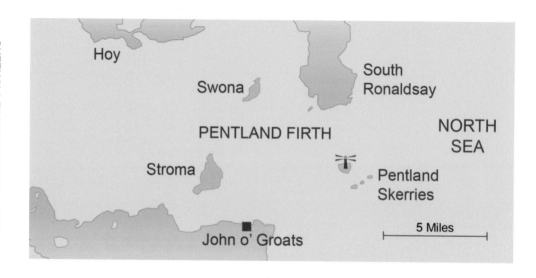

Hoy

Swona

South
Ronaldsay

PENTLAND FIRTH

NORTH
SEA

Stroma

Pentland
Skerries

John o' Groats

5 Miles

Thomas Smith, the first Engineer to the Northern Lighthouse Board, completed two lighthouse towers on Muckle Skerry, the largest of the Pentland Skerries, in 1794. Orkney masons built one tower 80 feet high, the other 60, and set them 60 feet apart. In the early days of lighthouse construction there were no revolving or flashing lights, so each tower provided a fixed light comprising an array of 66 oil lamps equipped with parabolic reflectors. Robert Stevenson, the young assistant who superintended the construction, succeeded Thomas Smith as Engineer to the Board in 1807 and rebuilt the lighthouse in more permanent form between 1821 and 1830, raising the larger tower to 100 feet. The optics were upgraded to more efficient refracting lenses in 1847, and in 1895 the light on the lower tower was discontinued and replaced by a foghorn. Robert's lighthouse tower is now listed as a building of architectural and historical interest.

The map shows the Pentland Skerries in relation to the Scottish mainland and two large southern Orkney Islands, South Ronaldsay and Hoy. Muckle Skerry has an area of about 420 acres and rises to a modest height of 66 feet above the sea. There are no human inhabitants but it attracts plenty of seals, and about a thousand pairs of arctic terns in the breeding season. Vessels passing through the Pentland Firth must beware of the small islands of Swona and Stroma. The latter was given its own Stevenson lighthouse in 1896.

Hazardous tidal races, eddies, and skerries in the Pentland Firth have been dreaded by mariners for centuries. The Swilkie, a whirlpool generated by contrary tides off the northern tip of Stroma, is especially menacing. In the age of sail, to enter Hell's Mouth at the eastern end of the firth in gale conditions, especially with wind and tide in opposition, was considered little short of signing one's death warrant.

Installation of a double light on the Pentland Skerries was intended to open up the Pentland Firth to sailing ships passing between the southern North Sea and the Atlantic Ocean, in place of longer routes around Orkney and Shetland. Yet even a lighthouse could not prevent tragedies. The Northern Lighthouse Board could illuminate the firth as brightly as Edinburgh on Hogmanay, but it could hardly stop mariners from risking their necks. Indeed it can be argued – as it was by some back in 1794 – that the new lighthouse, by tempting ships into the Pentland Firth, was endangering rather than saving lives at sea. In fairness to the Board, it never made any claims about preventing shipwrecks; its aim was to inform sailors of their whereabouts and act as a warning. The paramount duty of its employees was not to rescue sailors in distress, but to keep the lights burning, night after night without fail.

Nevertheless there were occasional heroic efforts by lighthouse staff to attempt rescues. In 1871 the Royal Humane Society awarded a bronze medal to Donald Montgomery, assistant keeper on the Pentland Skerries, for rescuing a boy in the 'boiling tideway' east of Muckle Skerry after the crew of the *Good Design* of Wick had abandoned ship. In 1884 nine men died when the *Vicksburg* of Leith went aground on the Skerries, but the keepers managed to rescue twelve others at huge personal risk.

In more recent times the extraordinary dangers of the Pentland Firth in foul weather caused the tragic loss of the Longhope lifeboat and its eight-man crew in 1969. They set off from Hoy at 8 p.m. on 23 March in their 48-foot steel craft, in response to an SOS from the 2,300-ton Liberian vessel *Irene* which was drifting out of control near South Ronaldsay in a

Force 9 gale. The weather off Hoy was appalling, with bad visibility and snow flurries, and as the lifeboat battled against the tidal race she was overwhelmed by maelstrom conditions. Nobody ever discovered exactly what happened, but she was found the next afternoon floating upside down at the western end of the firth, 15 miles from the Pentland Skerries Lighthouse, with seven bodies on board. By a cruel irony the entire crew of the *Irene* had been rescued – not by a lifeboat, nor even in the Pentland Firth, but by breeches buoy from the northeast shore of South Ronaldsay.

COPINSAY LIGHTHOUSE

Engineer: David A. Stevenson   *Year established*: 1915
Location: The small island of Copinsay, about 2 miles
off the east coast of Mainland, Orkney
Latitude: 58° 53.8' N   *Longitude*: 2° 40.3' W
Nominal range: 21 nautical miles   *Elevation*: 260 feet (79 metres)
Character: Flashing (5) white every 30 seconds   *Automated*: 1991

Copinsay Lighthouse (NLB).

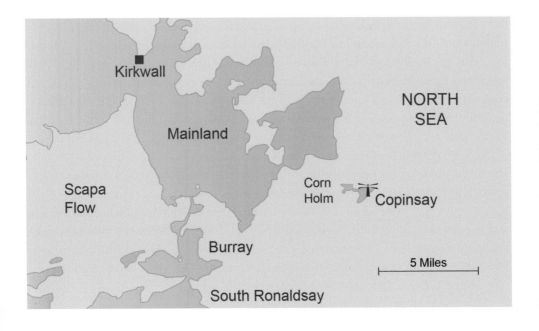

Our next lighthouse is perched high on the small island of Copinsay, about 17 miles NNE of the Pentland Skerries. It was built in 1915 by David A. Stevenson, a grandson of Robert. The main reason for this addition to the lighthouse chain was the increasing use of Scapa Flow by the Royal Navy during World War I. As the map shows, Copinsay was well placed to illuminate the eastern access to Scapa Flow before the Churchill Barriers were built between Burray and Mainland in World War II. Today, it alerts North Sea shipping to Orkney's eastern coastline and aids navigation towards the harbour at Kirkwall.

The white tower of the lighthouse is 52 feet tall and perches about 200 feet above the sea on vertical cliffs, which are a striking feature of Copinsay's east side. The lighthouse was fitted with a Stevenson refractor lens rotating on a bath of mercury to produce a group-flashing white light. The original paraffin lamp was of the Tilley type, manufactured by Chance Brothers, and used air pressure to supply the burner with vaporised fuel. The lantern, revolving apparatus, and parapet were provided by James Milne and Son of Edinburgh. A fog horn was operated by compressed air powered by three Kelvin diesel engines, giving 4 blasts every 60 seconds. The total cost of lighthouse and buildings was £13,400. Today Copinsay, like other Scottish lights, is remotely controlled from the Northern Lighthouse Board's headquarters in Edinburgh.

The island of Copinsay has an area of about 180 acres and is shaped like a giant wedge of cheese, tilting steeply up to the eastern cliffs. There are three islets off its low western side, of which the largest, Corn Holm, is joined to Copinsay by a long rock saddle exposed at low tide. In Victorian times the population was less than a dozen, but it peaked at 25 in the 1930s thanks to the resident farmer Mr Groat and his wife, their 13 children, the lightkeepers and their families, and a teacher who set up a classroom in the farmhouse. But by 1981 Copinsay was uninhabited. Then in 1991 a Staffordshire man bought the former lighthouse keeper's cottage for family holidays and was dismayed to be quoted nearly a million pounds by Scottish Hydroelectric to connect him to the electricity grid.

In 1972 money had been raised by public appeal to buy Copinsay as a memorial to the naturalist James Fisher, well known as a broadcaster, author, and ornithologist. The island, which is administered by the RSPB, has an extraordinary population of seabirds, especially the guillemots and kittiwakes that 'scatter like confetti' on the vertical cliffs below the lighthouse. There are also large numbers of razorbills, fulmars, eiders, and cormorants, with puffins and arctic terns on the adjacent islets. The RSPB manages the grass-topped island as cover for ground-nesting birds including the rare corncrake. As if all this were not enough, a huge colony of grey seals comes ashore in the autumn to pup.

Another notable feature is the Horse of Copinsay, a 60-foot grass-topped stack lying about half a mile off the northeast tip of the island. During easterly gales the sea is forced through a crevice in the rock known as Blaster Hole, producing a dramatic water jet that rises as much as 200 feet skywards. In former times the demand for grazing on Copinsay was so great that the islanders would somehow manhandle sheep to the top of the stack, and in springtime they would hoist a pig or two to gorge on the huge crop of seabird eggs. However it was no easy solution: the stack had grass to 'fatten one sheep, feed two, but starve three'. Life on Copinsay was never straightforward.

AUSKERRY LIGHTHOUSE

Engineers: David and Thomas Stevenson   *Year established: 1866*
Location: The small island of Auskerry, about 3 miles south of Stronsay
Latitude: 59° 01.6' N   Longitude: 2° 34.4' W
Nominal range: 18 nautical miles   Elevation: 110 feet (34 metres)
Character: Flashing white every 20 seconds   Automated: 1960s

Auskerry Lighthouse (NLB).

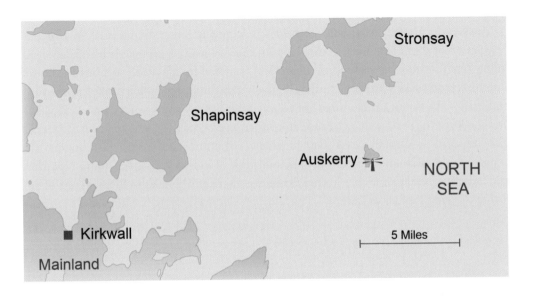

A low sandstone island with a rocky shoreline, Auskerry lies about 10 miles NNE of Copinsay and 14 miles ENE of the harbour at Kirkwall. Its white lighthouse tower was built in brick to an impressive height by David and Thomas Stevenson, raising the light well above the surrounding ocean. It is located on the southern tip of the island above a sharp inlet called Hunter's Geo, once a favourite spot for seal hunters.

The lighthouse station was designed to accommodate families, unusual on a small island set in vigorous tidal waters without safe anchorages or a guaranteed landing. In the early days attempts were made to deliver the mail and provisions monthly by fishing boat from Stronsay, 3 miles to the north across a dangerous sound. A unique signalling system, consisting of black disks displayed on the outside of the tower, was used to communicate with Stronsay, especially in emergency. 'Send midwife immediately' was among the list of coded messages.

Standing stones that raise their heads proudly above Auskerry's windswept landscape prove that it was inhabited as far back as the Stone Age. Later its remote beauty attracted Celtic Christians seeking solitude, and there is still a small ruined chapel on the east side. A few people eked out a living on the island in Victorian times, but by the 1930s only the lighthouse keepers remained. Three decades later the island was abandoned to the seals and a large colony of storm petrels, puffins, arctic terns, and black guillemots.

And then something remarkable occurred in the human story of Auskerry. A family bought the island in 1974 and started to raise a flock of rare North Ronaldsay sheep. A small stone bothy was extended step-by-step to create a family house with four bedrooms, and three young sons were given home schooling. In spite of the remoteness, and the winter weather that sometimes prevents contact with Stronsay for weeks on end, the family continues to develop the flock of sheep and market its fine wool products.

The sheep are extraordinary. An ancient Orkney breed farmed by original settlers, their fleeces are said to have lined the beds in the Stone Age houses of Skara Brae. Today the majority are kept on Orkney's most northerly island, North Ronaldsay, but flocks have been started elsewhere and a rare breed society was formed in 1997. For more about this unique breed, see the North Ronaldsay Lighthouse section.

Auskerry's nearest neighbour Stronsay is a much larger island with a resident population of about 350. Back in the late 18th century many local people were employed in the kelp industry, harvesting and processing seaweed for glass and soap manufacture. But the activity was dwarfed by the developing herring industry, which peaked in the 19th and early 20th centuries. Hundreds of fishing boats, many from as far away as Holland and the Firths of Forth and Tay, used Stronsay as a seasonal port, and an army of herring girls travelled up Orkney's east coast to follow, salt and pack the silver fish, much of it exported to Russia and Germany. By the outbreak of World War II the boom was over, and today it is hard to imagine Stronsay's main settlement, Whitehall Village, as one of the former herring capitals of Europe.

Start Point Lighthouse

Engineer: Robert Stevenson   *Year established*: 1806
Location: Eastern tip of the island of Sanday
Latitude: 59° 16.6' N   *Longitude*: 2° 22.6' W
Nominal range: 24 nautical miles   *Height of tower*: 82 feet (25 metres)
Character: Flashing (2) white every 20 seconds   Automated: 1962

Start Point Lighthouse (NLB).

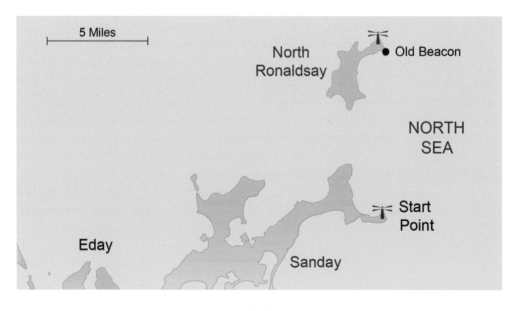

Start Point is a tidal islet at the eastern tip of the island of Sanday, about 19 miles north of Auskerry as the seabird flies. We are now approaching the northern reaches of the Orkney archipelago, dangerous territory for shipping en route between the North Sea and North Atlantic. By the 18th century Sanday and its neighbour North Ronaldsay were exacting a tragic toll on vessels and their crews, and the area was prioritised for attention by the newly formed Northern Lighthouse Board and its Engineer, Thomas Smith. The first lighthouse was erected on North Ronaldsay in 1789; a second building, an unlit masonry tower, was placed on Start Point in 1802. But the dual arrangement failed to prevent shipwrecks, especially on Sanday, and the NLB Commissioners decided to give Start Point a powerful new lighthouse, with accommodation for principal and assistant lightkeepers and their families. Built by Robert Stevenson, it was lit in 1806. Three years later Thomas Smith's original light on North Ronaldsay was decommissioned.

The Start Point Lighthouse was, quite literally, revolutionary. It was the first Scottish lighthouse to be equipped with a revolving light, producing a unique and distinctive pattern of flashes. It was subsequently fitted with a magnificent Fresnel lens system consisting of a set of highly polished glass elements set in a brass framework. Adding to its unique appearance by night, the tower was repainted in 1915 with black and white vertical stripes to give it a zebra appearance by day. Start Point intends to be highly visible.

Construction of the lighthouse on the flat and relatively accessible land of Start Point went smoothly and was completed in seven months, but disaster beckoned as the principal mason and his assistants prepared to return home. They made for Stromness, Orkney's second port, and embarked on a schooner bound for Leith, the port of Edinburgh. The vessel sailed with a fair wind and got within sight of Kinnaird Head Lighthouse on Scotland's east coast; but a tremendous south-easterly gale forced her back towards Orkney as darkness fell. The next step was to prove fatal. The schooner, no doubt guided by the recently built Pentland Skerries Lighthouse, entered Hell's Mouth and, failing to reach a proper anchorage, smashed against the isle of Flotta at the southern end of Scapa Flow. The weather was terrible, rescue was impossible, and those who managed to hold on to the rigging were frozen to death by daybreak. The sole survivor was a cabin boy.

Sanday, one of Orkney's larger islands with an area of about 20 square miles, supported a population of around 2,000 in the late 19th century. In recent years it has stabilised at about 500. Most of the island is treeless, windswept, and barely above sea level, but its light fertile soils make the farms among the most prosperous in Orkney. Seen from the air, Sanday's flat landscape has been described as resembling a 'gigantic fossilised bat', with several peninsulas radiating out from a central area and a coastline indented by shallow bays and beautiful sandy beaches. But mariners feared the island greatly, because it was almost invisible from the sea in murky weather conditions and many vessels simply ran into it. There is no peat on Sanday so wrecks were traditionally prized by islanders for their wood, used for fuel or fashioned into useful items for homes and farms. The new lighthouse may have been a godsend to sailors, but it was far from popular with some of the locals.

NORTH RONALDSAY LIGHTHOUSE

Engineers: *Thomas Smith; Alan Stevenson*   Years established: *1789; 1853*
Location: *Northeast tip of the island of North Ronaldsay*
Latitude: *59° 23.3' N*   Longitude: *2° 22.9' W*
Nominal range: *24 nautical miles*   Elevation: *139 feet (42 metres)*
Character: *Flashing white every 10 seconds*   Automated: *1998*

North Ronaldsay Lighthouse (NLB).

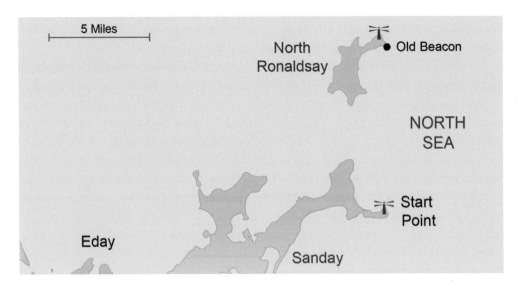

The Northern Isles and their lighthouses

In 1789 Thomas Smith, assisted by Robert Stevenson, completed a 70-foot tower of local undressed stone on North Ronaldsay. Lit by a cluster of oil lamps with copper reflectors, it was the Northern Lighthouse Board's third lighthouse, after Kinnaird Head in Aberdeenshire and the Mull of Kintyre in Argyllshire. In 1802 it was complemented by an unlit stone beacon erected at Start Point on nearby Sanday. However the combination proved ineffective at preventing shipwrecks, especially on Sanday, so it was decided to build a powerful new light at Start Point, which was lit in 1806.

At this stage the original stone beacon at Start Point became redundant, so it was demolished and the great stone ball that had decorated its summit was shipped to North Ronaldsay. The original light on North Ronaldsay was extinguished in 1809 and its lantern replaced by the stone ball, converting it into an unlit beacon. Two hundred years later the 'Old Beacon' was in a sorry state; but it has recently been restored for tourist inspection, and stands proud once again as the oldest surviving lighthouse tower in Scotland.

As the years passed the tragic catalogue of shipwrecks on Orkney's far northern shores continued, so in the early 1850s the Commissioners decided to give North Ronaldsay a powerful new lighthouse of its own. Robert Stevenson's eldest son Alan was by now Engineer to the Board and he was determined to do things properly. His majestic 130-foot tower, the one we see today, is the highest land-based lighthouse ever built in the British Isles. There was no suitable local stone in North Ronaldsay, so he settled on a brick construction to ease the problems of transport and handling.

The new lighthouse was built a few hundred yards from the Old Beacon, at the extreme northeast tip of the island, giving maximum warning of local reefs and especially the dangerous Seal Skerry immediately offshore. The contract for the tower was awarded to an Edinburgh builder who first had to construct a stone jetty for importing bricks and other materials. The tower's height became a source of wonder to locals used to a low-lying island just a few feet above the surrounding ocean. In 1889 the red brick tower was given two white horizontal bands as a unique day mark, visible, in clear weather, from far out to sea.

In recent years the remarkable history of North Ronaldsay's two historic lighthouses, and their attraction for tourists, has been recognised by converting former keepers' cottages into a visitor centre with a café and shop, holiday accommodation, and a woollen mill for spinning the fleeces of the island's famous seaweed-eating sheep.

The island's 1,700 acres were extensively cultivated and studded with cottages in Victorian times, supporting a farming population of about 500. It declined steadily through the 20th century but is currently stable at around 60. The small but resourceful community keeps cattle and, most famously, several thousand North Ronaldsay sheep that graze the foreshore, going far out onto the rocks for seaweed exposed by the ebbing tide. The animals alternately graze and ruminate at times of day and night determined by the tides. Their digestive systems have apparently adapted to this curious lifestyle. The meat is dark, lean, and rich in minerals, considered a delicacy and best in the winter months when it is most needed. Although the fleeces are rough and hairy on the outside, they are as soft as cashmere underneath. Apart from the lambing season the animals are kept off the inland pasture by a remarkable 12-mile long sheep dyke stretching right around the coast. Completed in the mid-19th century, it is now classed as a scheduled monument.

Fair Isle

We now cross 27 miles of wild ocean to a small island with a big history. Fair Isle lies roughly midway between Orkney and Shetland and is home to two Stevenson lighthouses, set in dramatic locations at opposite ends of the island.

Fair Isle, administratively part of Shetland, is the most remote island in Scotland with a significant population. The numbers were decimated by smallpox in 1701 but recovered slowly, to peak at 380 in 1861. The following year a third of its people emigrated to Nova Scotia, adding to the sorry history of the Highland Clearances that affected so much of Scotland in Victorian times. Numbers continued to fall so that by 1950 there was talk of complete evacuation, but the purchase of the island in 1954 by the National Trust for Scotland heralded a new era. Today a small but resilient community of about 70 cares for a spectacular island that has won many accolades, national and international, for its natural beauty, pristine environment, and stunning wildlife.

Popular imagination, at least in Britain, tends to associate Fair Isle with three things: a special brand of knitwear, full of vibrant patterns and colours; a sea area that figures daily in the BBC's shipping forecasts; and, among bird lovers, a reputation as one of the most exciting destinations in the British Isles.

Fair Isle knitwear has been a traditional cottage industry of the island's womenfolk for generations. The unique style began when local knitters discovered that they could strand fine woollen yarns into a double layer to produce warm and durable yet lightweight garments, suitable for their families or for bartering with passing ships. Today a small band of dedicated enthusiasts keeps the tradition going on hand-frame machines, producing

Two lighthouses may just be seen in this aerial view: Fair Isle South in the foreground, Fair Isle North in the far distance (photo: Tommy Hyndman).

garments of the highest quality that sell around the world. Although Fair Isle knitwear has become internationally famous – and widely copied – it is still possible to buy and treasure the genuine article.

It may seem surprising that one of the sea areas in BBC shipping forecasts is named after a small remote island. But 'Fair Isle' embraces all the waters around Orkney and Shetland, including substantial stretches of the North Atlantic to the west and the North Sea to the east. The island owes its fame, proclaimed four times a day on the radio, to its position roughly midway between its larger neighbours, the centre of its own universe, set in sparkling but often stormy seas.

Fair Isle's spectacular birdlife has grown in fame ever since George Waterston, a former owner of the island, set up a bird observatory in 1948. Expanded and rebuilt in 1969, it provides much of the island's visitor accommodation. This is one of the best places in Europe for observing rare birds blown off course by contrary winds, or on major migration routes, especially in September and October. An astonishing total of some 350 resident and migrant species has been recorded, more than any other place in the British Isles, and over the years the observatory has contributed significantly to ornithological research as well as attracting visitors from around the world.

Fair Isle South Lighthouse

Engineers: David A. and Charles Stevenson   Year established: 1892
Location: The southern tip of Fair Isle
Latitude: 59° 30.9' N   Longitude: 1° 39.2' W
Nominal range: 22 nautical miles   Elevation: 105 feet (32 metres)
Character: Flashing (4) white every 30 seconds   Automated: 1998

Fair Isle South Lighthouse (Geograph/Julian Paren).

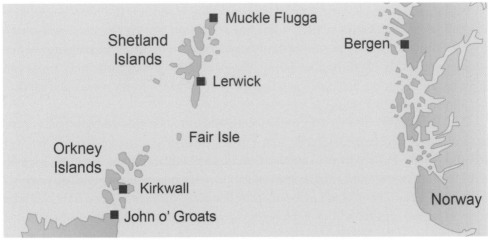

Fair Isle lies roughly midway between the Orkney and Shetland Islands.

On 31 March 1998 Princess Anne, patron of the Northern Lighthouse Board, visited Fair Isle and met the final shift of keepers on the Fair Isle South Lighthouse. She also unveiled a plaque to commemorate 'the invaluable service of generations of lightkeepers from 1787 to 1998'. It was both a celebration and a sad farewell, marking over two centuries of service throughout Scotland. Fair Isle South was the last of the Board's lights to be automated.

The lighthouse is one of a pair designed for Fair Isle over a century earlier by David A. and Charles Stevenson, Engineers to the Board and grandsons of Robert Stevenson. The southern end of the island is relatively low lying, so Fair Isle South had to be built fairly high to give an adequate range. The white tower rises 73 feet above ground level and there are 96 steps to the top. The light was supplemented by a fog horn powered by compressed air, giving two 1.5-second blasts every 60 seconds.

Fair Isle's two lighthouses formed a valuable addition to the chain of lights signposting the way past Orkney and Shetland. In some ways they were a surprisingly late addition because the island's threat to shipping was hardly new; as far back as 1588 scattered remnants of the Spanish Armada, fleeing home around the northern coasts of Orkney and Shetland, had gambled with its rocks. One of the biggest warships was wrecked, and more than 200 sailors, weak and starving, were taken in and looked after by the islanders before being firmly escorted away to Shetland and eventually repatriated.

Fickle and sometimes violent seas around Orkney, Shetland, and Fair Isle ensured that, lit or unlit, the islands would continue to exact their price. One of the most notorious incidents, known as the Fair Isle Disaster, occurred in September 1897, five years after the South Light had been established. Four small boats headed out to sea in fine weather to barter with passing vessels 12 miles offshore, but the weather worsened rapidly and two of them, *Spray* and *Star of Hope,* failed to make it back in gale-force winds and high seas. The islanders gathered overnight on the shoreline in appalling weather, hoping desperately for good news, but *Spray* went down without trace and *Star of Hope* limped home the next day with three bodies aboard. One was a 14-year-old boy who had perished at the tiller. The disaster so shocked the nation that a large support fund was raised; but Fair Isle was left with 24 fatherless children, 4 bereaved widows, and 2 heartbroken grandmothers.

Fair Isle South was also the scene of tragedy during World War II. Enemy bombs were dropped on the lighthouse in 1941, killing the wife of the assistant keeper; and again in 1942, killing the wife and daughter of the principal keeper and setting the buildings on fire. A colleague on Fair Isle North Lighthouse struggled 3 miles through gale-force winds and snow to help repair the damaged light, and was later rewarded with a medal. The incident is commemorated by a plaque on the station's boundary wall.

If all this makes gloomy reading, we should remember that Fair Isle was by no means alone in its catalogue of disasters, especially in the days of sail. All seas around Scottish reefs and islands, from the Firth of Forth to the Northern Isles and westward to the Hebrides, were extremely dangerous in rough weather and at night. This was, of course, the principal reason for setting up the Northern Lighthouse Board in the first place. But lighthouses could never calm the seas, prevent occasional misjudgements by captains and crews, or ban attacks from the air.

We live in gentler times today and it is possible to visit Fair Isle South, climb its tower, marvel at the views, and even stay in the former keepers' accommodation.

FAIR ISLE NORTH LIGHTHOUSE

Engineers: David A. and Charles Stevenson   Year established: 1892
Location: Close to the northern tip of Fair Isle
Latitude: 59° 33.1' N   Longitude: 1° 36.5' W
Nominal range: 22 nautical miles   Elevation: 262 feet (80 metres)
Character: Flashing (2) white every 30 seconds   Automated: 1983

Fair Isle North Lighthouse (Geograph/Julian Paren).

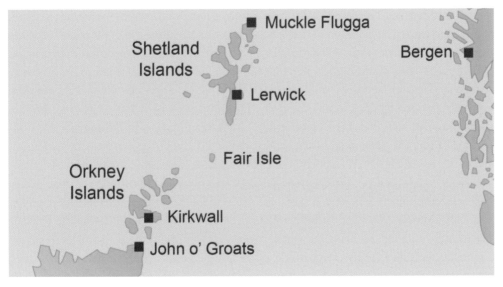

Fair Isle in relation to Orkney and Shetland.

Fair Isle's 1,900 acres rise to a maximum of 712 feet above the sea and have a highly distinctive outline. Relatively gentle, fertile land in the south contains most of the buildings, dwellings, and crofts, taking advantage of the modest shelter provided by a shallow valley. But the north, with high sandstone cliffs and rocky moorland, is altogether wilder. The famous bird observatory is roughly in the middle. Apart from birds, no less than 240 species of flowering plant have been recorded in Fair Isle's dramatic, and sometimes unforgiving, landscape.

Fair Isle North Lighthouse is perched on an isolated rocky promontory close to the northern tip of the island. It was completed by David A. and Charles Stevenson in the same year as Fair Isle South, with a lower tower but similar equipment. The original light was a paraffin lamp, started with a vaporiser and refilled by hand pump. It was fitted with a new form of silk mantle described as 'autoform', shapeless when first lit but ballooning up into a spherical shape. The Fresnel lens had four sections with double 'bulls eyes', and rotated once every two minutes to give a character of two flashes in quick succession followed by a 30-second pause. The apparatus was carried by a table moving on rollers, rotated by gearing and driven by weights. If a keeper failed to rewind the weights in time, he was alerted by alarm bells both inside and outside the lighthouse. Later the station also emitted fog signals consisting of 3 short blasts every 45 seconds, powered by air compressors driven by diesel engines.

Like its sister lighthouse on the south of the island, Fair Isle North suffered two raids by enemy aircraft in 1941, which damaged the buildings and boundary wall but, fortunately, caused no human casualties. The assistant keeper had a very narrow escape in the first raid, but managed to trudge through snow and gale-force winds to give help at the more seriously damaged south light.

The automation of Scottish lighthouses really got under way in the 1960s in response to the high costs of manning and improvements in automatic control technology. By the early 1980s the Northern Lighthouse Board was completing its automation of major lights, and Fair Isle North was a priority due to deterioration of its buildings, difficult access, and the social isolation of keepers stuck out on the north tip of the island. The old clock mechanism was removed and replaced by a gearless rotating pedestal operating on 12 volts DC. The paraffin light was replaced by sealed-beam electric lamps, mounted in two arrays to give the correct character, and supplied by large-capacity nickel cadmium batteries charged by generators. Today the lighthouse is largely left to its own devices, monitored from the Northern Lighthouse Board's headquarters in Edinburgh.

Fair Isle may be Scotland's most remote inhabited island but it is far from lacking modern facilities. An extremely important one for a small community is, of course, electricity. The island is a long way from the national grid, so a 60kW wind turbine was installed in 1982 as a community initiative. It has some claim to be the first commercial wind energy scheme in Europe. A second turbine, rated at 100kW, was installed in 1996. The Fair Isle Electricity Company, probably the smallest electricity utility in the British Isles, provides a reliable electricity supply thanks to an extremely generous supply of nature's 'free fuel', backed up when necessary by diesel generators. It sets its charges to encourage electricity consumption when the wind blows hard and uses any excess to heat the island's buildings.

Apart from about 30 dwellings and the bird observatory, Fair Isle currently has four public buildings in regular use, five active workshops, and several cottages available for holiday lets. The islanders derive their livelihood from diverse occupations including crofting, fishing, keeping sheep, tourism, knitting, arts and crafts, and serving on the island's mailboat. They are a resourceful lot.

SHETLAND

The Shetland archipelago begins 24 miles across the sea from Fair Isle. Most people in mainland Britain fail to appreciate that it is closer to Bergen than to Aberdeen. No wonder the Norse influence, already strong in Orkney, is even more pronounced in Shetland, where the locals combine a delightful hospitality with a proud independence, a strong musical tradition, and a way of farming that has produced the world-famous Shetland ponies and sheepdogs.

There are about 100 islands, mostly with Norse names, strung out roughly north–south over a distance of 50 miles. With a total area of 570 square miles and a jagged coastline 1,680 miles long, they form the last barrier separating the North Sea from the Atlantic Ocean. It is said that nowhere in Shetland is further than 3 miles from the sea. There are 16 inhabited islands with a total population of about 23,000, similar to Orkney, but the human population is greatly outnumbered by sheep and vastly outnumbered by seabirds. Lerwick, the capital, is home to about 7,000 people.

Perhaps the most obvious physical difference between Orkney and Shetland, at least to the visitor, lies in the landscape. Whereas most of Orkney is flat and fertile, with plenty of good land for crops and livestock, Shetland is far more rugged. Orkney's geology is largely Old Red Sandstone with slab-shaped profiles and cliffs mainly limited to the Atlantic coast. Shetland's rocks are largely Precambrian with undulating profiles; cliffs intrude and the landscape, often majestic, has a more primitive quality.

The Jarlshof settlement on Mainland, Shetland (Geograph/M. J. Richardson).

The famous broch on the Isle of Mousa, Shetland (Wikipedia).

Hunter-gatherers settled in Shetland during the Stone Age. As in Orkney, there are some remarkable prehistoric monuments, including the Jarlshof settlement near the southern tip of Mainland, which dates from about 2500BC and is considered one of the most important archaeological sites in the British Isles. It lies close to Shetland's historic lighthouse at Sumburgh Head. Another famous relic is the Broch of Mousa, the best preserved and tallest round tower still standing in Europe, built on a small island south of Lerwick in about 100BC.

The first written references to Shetland were left by the Romans, at a time when it was inhabited by Picts. Later, like Orkney, Shetland was taken over by Vikings as an ideal launching pad for wider conquests. They imposed Norse culture for 600 years. The islands became part of Scotland in the 15th century and for the next 300 years there was a great deal of contact with the countries and cities of the Hanseatic League; Shetlanders sold salted fish to German merchants in Bergen, Bremen and Hamburg in exchange for grain, cloth, and beer. However the 1707 Act of Union that created the United Kingdom prohibited German merchants from trading with Shetland, a cruel blow to its economy which entered a dark era, including the terrible effects of the clearances by landowners who preferred sheep to people.

In modern times, Shetland's historic links with Norway were rekindled during World War II when a naval unit, the 'Shetland Bus', was set up by Britain's Special Operations Executive. About 30 camouflaged fishing boats sailed, often under cover of darkness, to support the Norwegian resistance against Nazi occupation, transferring agents in and out of Norway, and supplying them with weapons, radios and other supplies. The operation was coordinated from Shetland by British army personnel.

Discovery of North Sea oil in the 1970s launched Shetland fully into the modern world. The Sullom Voe oil and liquefied gas terminal, built between 1975 and 1981, handles production from oilfields in the North Sea and East Shetland Basin, exporting it by tanker around the world. The Shetland Islands Council negotiated a robust deal with the oil companies, insisting that all pipelines terminate at a single site to minimise environmental damage; and rather than spending the income like the rest of the UK, the council was wise enough to set up an oil fund on the Norwegian pattern and invest for the future of the islands. The Norse influence continues.

Sumburgh Head Lighthouse

Engineer: Robert Stevenson   Year established: 1821
Location: The southern tip of Mainland, Shetland
Latitude: 59° 51.2' N   Longitude: 1° 16.5' W
Nominal range: 23 nautical miles   Elevation: 299 feet (91 metres)
Character: Flashing (3) white every 30 seconds   Automated: 1991

Sumburgh Head Lighthouse (NLB).

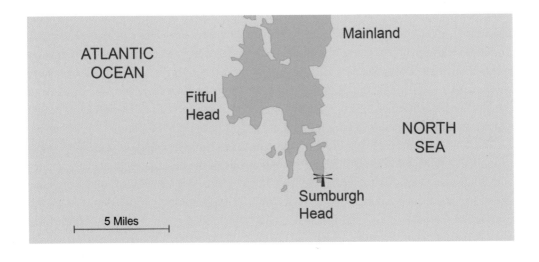

Flying into Sumburgh Airport at the southern tip of Shetland, you can expect a good view of the lighthouse perched on its dramatic headland. Further attractions on the ground will repay any time you can give them: an excellent visitor centre based in and around the lighthouse, an RSPB nature reserve with many thousands of breeding seabirds and dramatic cliff scenery, and two archaeological sites of major historical importance.

Sumburgh Head Lighthouse overlooks a stretch of water known as the Roost, where two tidal streams meet with dramatic and sometimes treacherous effect. The lighthouse, Shetland's first, was built by Robert Stevenson following a tour of inspection and survey he made in 1814. Its construction, featuring walls of double thickness to keep out the damp, was contracted to a builder from Peterhead in Aberdeenshire, and the light first shone out on 15 January 1821, ten years after Robert had completed his Bell Rock masterpiece in the North Sea off the coast by Arbroath.

The lighthouse was initially equipped with a stationary light based on reflectors and fuelled by whale oil, but a rotating lens and paraffin lamp were later substituted and by 1976 electricity had taken over from paraffin. The Fresnel lens, a majestic first-order system of the type pioneered by the French inventor Augustin Fresnel, was the largest of various standard sizes installed in Scottish lighthouses, with a diameter of 8 feet 6 inches. In 1914 the rotating mechanism was upgraded to one floating on a bath of mercury, giving the 3-ton apparatus exceptional stability and frictionless movement. In 1952 the lighthouse engine room was equipped with three large Kelvin K2 diesel engines driving air compressors to power the station's foghorn. These have recently been restored to their former glory, and form part of the lighthouse's many visitor attractions.

Robert Stevenson, Engineer to the Northern Lighthouse Board, had a very clear view of the responsibilities of lighthouse keepers and demanded extremely high standards. He viewed the lighthouse service as requiring military precision, and gave careless work or shoddy housekeeping short shrift. The overriding objective was, of course, to keep the light working night after night, year after year, without fail. About the worst thing a keeper could do was fall asleep on watch, allowing the light to fail or the revolving mechanism to run down. Probably the worst case in Scottish lighthouse history occurred at Sumburgh Head in 1871 when two men, both guilty of the offence, agreed not to report one another. However their conspiracy was detected and they were immediately dismissed – even though one of them had given 23 years' service as a principal keeper.

Such human problems were eliminated, at least in theory, when Sumburgh Head was automated in 1991. The keepers left the station, and the cottages and outbuildings were subsequently acquired by the Shetland Amenity Trust. In 2014 Princess Anne, patron of the Northern Lighthouse Board, officially opened the restored site as a world-class visitor centre, with the aim of developing tourism at the southern tip of Shetland.

The RSPB's Sumburgh Nature Reserve, close to the lighthouse, is one of its most accessible seabird colonies in Shetland, as well as one of the best places to observe whales and dolphins. Nearby is the Iron Age and Norse settlement of Jarlshof, with a history stretching back over 3,000 years. It includes Iron Age homes, a broch, and a Viking fish factory discovered in 1905 at the sea edge after a storm; the village sits somewhat incongruously near the main road and airport. Subsequent airport expansion led to another major discovery half a mile away: in 1975, during construction of an access road, a stunning Iron Age village and broch was uncovered at Old Scatness – an 'undisturbed, pristine time-capsule' which is also cared for by the Shetland Amenity Trust.

BRESSAY LIGHTHOUSE

Engineers: David and Thomas Stevenson Year established: 1858
Location: Island of Bressay, near Lerwick
Latitude: 60° 7.2' N Longitude: 1° 7.3' W
Nominal range: 23 nautical miles Elevation: 105 feet (32 metres)
Character: Flashing (2) white every 20 seconds Automated: 1989

Bressay Lighthouse (Wikipedia/Hajotthu).

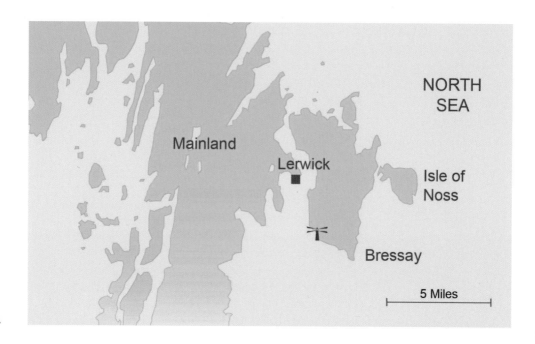

For over 150 years the 'Bressa Light' guided vessels towards Shetland's main harbour at Lerwick, a welcoming landmark and quite often a saviour from disaster. Today the original lighthouse and buildings, completed by David and Thomas Stevenson in 1858, offer a fine location for holidays on tranquil Bressay, a ten-minute ferry ride from Shetland's bustling capital.

The lighthouse nestles on a promontory below high cliffs at Kirkabister Ness on the south-western edge of Bressay. It was electrified in 1967 and automated in 1989. Six years later the keepers' cottages and outbuildings were purchased from the Northern Lighthouse Board by the Shetland Amenity Trust, with the aim of creating a heritage centre and visitor accommodation, while leaving the light in the care of the Board. However there was a change of plan in 2012, following a Merchant Shipping Act which defined the light's location as being within the limits of Lerwick Harbour. At this point the Board decommissioned the Stevenson light with its 23-mile range, and the Lerwick Port Authority installed an adjacent 10-mile LED light with the same character. The Board's involvement with Bressay was now over, and the old lighthouse tower joined the other buildings as part of the Shetland Amenity Trust's visitor experience.

Bressay's 11 square miles support a population of about 400, just a twentieth that of Lerwick a mile away across the Sound. In fact they depend upon each other. Lerwick's excellent harbour would never have been developed without the shelter offered by Bressay, and the roofs of many of its houses would be less secure without the 'slates' made of Bressay's old red sandstone. On the other hand Bressay owes much of its livelihood and amenities to Shetland's capital, with its 5-star museum, leisure centre, restaurants, bars, and shopping facilities. Today, Lerwick comes across as a bustling cosmopolitan seaport, welcoming visitors arriving by land and sea, with a vibrant cultural life including the world-famous 'Up Helly Aa' fire festival, the Shetland Folk Festival, and numerous musical events including a Fiddle Frenzy.

It was not always so. The fine anchorage in Bressay Sound was known to the Vikings, but it was Dutch fishermen who developed it as a port in the 15th century. Their large two-masted craft crowded into the sound in huge numbers, often accompanied by uninvited men-of-war. It is said that locals could cross from Mainland to Bressay by stepping on Dutch boats, which exported Scottish herring throughout the western world. Charles I tried to control them with his Royal Navy, and after minor hostilities the Dutch agreed to pay annual fees and obey the rules. Sadly, the social and economic structure of the Scottish islands at the time prevented locals from owning large fishing boats and joining in the bonanza, so the vast wealth of Shetland's seas was exploited by foreigners. The grubby hamlet of Lerwick started as little more than a servicing centre for their boats and took a long time to develop, especially since it was demolished by court orders in 1615 and 1625, attacked by the Dutch in 1673, and set ablaze by the French in 1702. Today's flourishing scene makes it hard to imagine Lerwick's past tribulations.

Back on Bressay there is a wealth of wildlife including moorland and sea birds, grey and common seals, and occasional cetaceans. The island abounds in archaeological sites, freshwater lochs with good trout, and stunning cliff scenery. On a clear day most of Shetland is visible from its highest hill, the Ward of Bressay (742 feet). To the south you should be able to make out Sumburgh Head and, with luck, Fair Isle; to the northeast, Out Skerries, our next destination.

Out Skerries Lighthouse

Engineers: David and Thomas Stevenson   Year established: 1854
Location: Bound Skerry, the most easterly islet of the Out Skerries archipelago
Latitude: 60° 25.5' N   Longitude: 0° 43.7' W
Nominal range: 20 nautical miles   Elevation: 144 feet (44 metres)
Character: Flashing white every 20 seconds   Automated: 1972

Out Skerries Lighthouse (Geograph/Julian Paren).

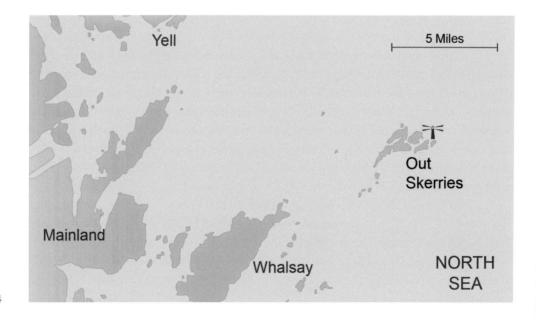

The small archipelago of Out Skerries must be about the most remote place to live in the whole of the British Isles. Some 25 miles north of Lerwick and well to the east of Shetland's main island chain, it is surrounded by dangerous waters studded with islets, skerries and stacks. A glance at the map shows why captains of vessels passing along the eastern seaboard of Shetland, or approaching from Bergen, must treat Out Skerries with the greatest respect. It is hardly surprising that the mid-19th-century British government, keen to protect the Royal Navy's northern squadron en route to the White Sea during the Crimean War, considered it a prime location for a new lighthouse.

Out Skerries' three main islands are Housay, Bruray, and Grunay. David and Thomas Stevenson, under pressure and in a hurry, built a temporary light on Grunay in September 1854. Four years later they completed a fine permanent lighthouse with a white tower 98 feet high; but rather than place it on Grunay, they moved to the islet of Bound Skerry at the archipelago's eastern extremity. Uninhabited and less accessible for the builder, it was better placed as a warning to mariners.

Like the two lighthouses on Fair Isle, Out Skerries received unwelcome attention from enemy aircraft during World War II. Suspected of housing a munitions store or even a factory, the station was machine-gunned in 1941, fortunately without causing injury; bombs were dropped in 1942, killing the mother of a boatman and causing extensive damage to buildings. The postmistress received a secret letter from the government, with instructions for the islanders in the event of an invasion; fortunately it was returned unopened at the end of the war.

The archipelago, known locally as the Skerries, has a long history of Neolithic, Iron Age, and Viking settlement, the latter indicated by hundreds of Norse place names. The word 'skerry' is derived from the Norse for a rocky islet, and Bound Skerry is believed to signify a small forerunner, often the first land sighted by vessels crossing the North Sea from Norway. Islanders ancient and modern have had to wrestle and work with the sea in all its moods, and fishing is still a mainstay of the local economy.

As you approach Out Skerries across a restless ocean, the sea cliffs, although not especially high, look impenetrable. But as the boat gets closer the narrow entrance of South Mouth opens up and beckons to a generous and almost landlocked harbour surrounded by the three main islands. The welcoming anchorage, extremely sheltered by Shetland standards, is surely the main reason why people choose to stay in such a remote spot.

The population peaked at 165 in 1891 but has now settled at about 70, living on Bruray and Housay. The two islands are linked by a concrete bridge built in 1957 and served by a solitary mile of road. Facilities include a school, two shops, a fish processing factory, a church and, surprisingly for such a law-abiding community, a police station. Low grassy hills provide grazing, and although the soil is thin it has traditionally been heaped into 'riggs' or mounds to allow cultivation of root vegetables. There is no fuel, but the islanders have longstanding rights to cut peat on neighbouring Whalsay. Ferries, often carrying birdwatchers to see the continental migrants that arrive on easterly winds, operate from Lerwick and the much closer harbour at Vidlin on Mainland.

MUCKLE FLUGGA LIGHTHOUSE

Engineers: Thomas and David Stevenson   Year established: 1858
Location: Muckle Flugga rock at the northern tip of Shetland
Latitude: 60° 51.3' N   Longitude: 0° 53.1' W
Nominal range: 22 nautical miles   Elevation: 217 feet (66 metres)
Character: Flashing (2) white every 20 seconds   Automated: 1995

Muckle Flugga Lighthouse (photo: Ian Cowe).

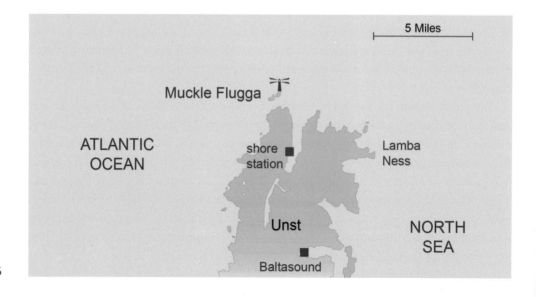

The final lighthouse in the chain that has brought us all the way from John o' Groats is, without doubt, the most extraordinary. Muckle Flugga, known by locals as 'the Flugga' and often referred to as Scotland's 'impossible lighthouse', clings to one of the most vicious rock outcrops in Northern Europe, assaulted by violent waves at the base and extreme winds at the summit.

A change of name from North Unst to Muckle Flugga in 1964 emphasised the lighthouse's dramatic location. A temporary light, established in 1854, was replaced by the permanent one in 1858 and upgraded to group-flashing in the 1920s. Lightkeeping duties expanded greatly in World War II as naval operations increased in the North Atlantic, and a keeper based in the shore station was employed relaying radio messages to and from colleagues on the rock. Electrification in the late 1960s freed up enough space for a new accommodation block to make the keepers' lives more comfortable, and the last of the dedicated breed left in 1995 when the most northerly lighthouse in the British Isles was automated.

The story of Muckle Flugga, our final destination, is so inspiring that it deserves a chapter of its own. In the meantime we explore the fascinating family background and personalities of the Stevenson engineers, and tap the experiences of two world-famous writers who, for very different reasons, left eye-witness accounts of their travels around the coasts of Scotland.

3 FAMILY TIES: THE REMARKABLE STEVENSONS

The Victorian era produced many great engineers. In some cases sons, and even grandsons, followed their fathers into the profession. One of the most remarkable examples is the Stevenson family of civil engineers who, from the first decade of the 19th century to the middle of the 20th, designed and built a pioneering series of Scottish lighthouses. Abroad, they lit the coastlines of New Zealand and Japan, and were consulted on lighthouses for Canada, India, Burma, and China. Their expertise was not confined to protecting lives at sea; they also built roads, bridges, harbours, and railways, extending the influence of Scottish engineering even more widely around the globe.

My own interest in Scottish Lighthouses began several years ago when a friend recommended Bella Bathurst's *The Lighthouse Stevensons* as a thoroughly worthwhile read. It was, to say the least, a revelation. Although I had often holidayed in the Highlands and Islands and noticed some fine lighthouses set in dramatic landscapes, I had no idea who had built them, or when. Bella's book changed all that and has led to a lasting fascination with the Stevenson story.

Robert Stevenson, founder of the dynasty, became internationally famous for his Bell Rock Lighthouse, perched on an isolated wave-washed rock in the North Sea some 50 miles northeast of Edinburgh. By the time it entered service in 1811 he was Engineer to the Northern Lighthouse Board, established in 1786 to light the coasts of Scotland and the Isle of Man. His sons Alan, David, and Thomas, and grandsons David Alan (generally known as David A.) and Charles, followed him into the lighthouse business and increased the tally of Scottish lights to around 200 in one of the most extraordinary sustained efforts by any family in the world of civil engineering.

Our journey from John o' Groats to the northern tip of Shetland has already taken us past 10 Stevenson lighthouses, and if we arrange them in chronological rather than geographical order, the progression of responsibility from father to sons and grandsons becomes clear:

- *Start Point*, Orkney (Robert, 1806)
- *Sumburgh Head*, Shetland (Robert, 1821)
- *North Ronaldsay*, Orkney (Alan, 1853)
- *Out Skerries*, Shetland (David and Thomas, 1854)
- *Bressay*, Shetland (David and Thomas, 1858)

The first two generations of Stevenson lighthouse engineers: Robert (1772–1850) and his sons Alan (1807–65), David (1815–86), and Thomas (1818–87) (Wikipedia).

- *Muckle Flugga*, Shetland (Thomas and David, 1858)
- *Auskerry*, Orkney (David and Thomas, 1866)
- *Fair Isle South* (David A. and Charles, 1892)
- *Fair Isle North* (David A. and Charles, 1892)
- *Copinsay*, Orkney (David A., 1915)

There is sometimes confusion about names and dates because responsibility for design and construction may have been shared, or passed from one man to another as a project developed (for example, Muckle Flugga); or an original light may have been upgraded or replaced (for example, North Ronaldsay). The above list gives the names of engineers credited by the Northern Lighthouse Board, and the dates when the lighthouses we see today were first lit.

The final destination for this story, the 'impossible lighthouse' on Muckle Flugga, gives us a special interest in the family background, personalities, and professional development of its engineers, Thomas and David Stevenson. Clearly this must involve their father Robert and older brother Alan. We should also include Thomas Smith (builder of the original Pentland Skerries Lighthouse), who was appointed by the Northern Lighthouse Board as its first Engineer and set the Stevensons on the path to lighthouse fame by taking on young Robert as an apprentice.

Robert was born in Glasgow in 1772 and had what can only be described as an unsettled childhood. His mother Jean Lillie seems to have eloped to marry his father (another Alan) sometime in 1771 when both were only 20. Tragedy ensured that Robert was to be their only child, for Jean's husband died of the mysterious 'night dews' two years later while on a business trip to the West Indies, leaving her and the toddler to fend for themselves.

Jean's next partner in the marriage stakes was James Hogg, a Glasgow merchant and manufacturer with somewhat dubious business interests. She produced two more sons, but he ran off to England with them, leaving her and little Robert in straitened circumstances. Determined to try and improve the six-year-old's chances, and recalling her own Edinburgh education, Jean moved back to the capital city and enrolled him in a charity school. Her ambition for him to become a minister in the Church of Scotland was thwarted by a continuing lack of funds, so that by the age of 14 he found himself apprenticed not to God but to an Edinburgh gunsmith.

Robert's turbulent early years began to settle when his mother attended church in Edinburgh's New Town and met the man who would become her third husband. Thomas Smith, born in 1752, had grown up in a village near Dundee on the Firth of Tay and suffered early tragedy when his father drowned in Dundee harbour. Accepting his devastated mother's advice that whatever trade he followed it had better be well away from water, he spent five years apprenticed to a Dundee metal worker before moving to Edinburgh and starting his own business manufacturing grates, lamps and metal paraphernalia for New Town's aspirational and expanding population.

Thomas Smith's combination of talent and ambition proved highly successful in business, but his personal life continued tragically. Infectious diseases were terrible tools of the Grim Reaper in the late 18th century and his first wife, a farmer's daughter, died of whooping cough soon after producing five children, three of whom died in infancy. He remarried and gained another daughter, but soon lost his second wife to consumption. Jean, who had known and befriended both his wives, moved into Thomas's household to help look after his young family and it is not hard to imagine that she was a willing match for a new engagement. The two grew closer, but before they could unite Jean had to track down her second husband, the errant James Hogg. A divorce – extremely rare and shocking in the social climate of the time – was eventually procured, and she married Thomas in 1787.

So by the age of 15 Robert Stevenson found himself the son of a thrice-married mother and the stepson of a man who had lost two previous wives. What he did not yet know was that in 1797 he would strengthen the Smith–Stevenson family network even further by marrying another Jean, the daughter of Thomas Smith by his first marriage. At this point Robert's stepfather also became his father-in-law and he had one Jean for a mother and another for a wife.

Many onlookers must have found the makeup of the Smith–Stevenson household strange, even quirky, but it worked. Both halves of the family adopted Edinburgh as their home city and the burgeoning New Town for their lifestyle. By 1803 Thomas Smith's success gave him the confidence to purchase a plot of land and build a family house large enough to accommodate the whole tribe in comfort and provide workshop space for experimenting with new designs.

The amalgamation of Smith and Stevenson interests not only stabilised Robert's home life, but opened up career possibilities beyond his wildest dreams or expectations. He left the gunsmith and was apprenticed to Thomas Smith's metalworking and lamp-making business, which was expanding to include the illumination of lighthouses using a novel form of reflector lamp. In due course his stepfather became his mentor and the two of them never looked back. Success with the reflector lamps meant that Thomas was appointed Engineer to the newly formed Northern Lighthouse Board in 1787; from 1791 onwards, at what nowadays seems the tender age of 19, Robert helped him build a superb series of pioneering lighthouses. The young man had discovered his vocation.

The breadth of experience gained by Robert Stevenson as a young man was extraordinary; summers spent travelling round the coast of Scotland, often to extremely remote locations and in considerable danger; winters back in Edinburgh, studying, experimenting, and planning. All this responsibility, willingly shouldered, meant that by his late teens Robert was a mature adult, still slightly uneasy with books and cultural activities but completely at home with practical engineering in stone, iron, and wood. He became a full partner with Smith in 1802, and when the latter retired as Engineer to the Board his own term in office began. He was to complete 14 Scottish lights of his own, including the world-famous Bell Rock (1811) and two on our list – Start Point (Orkney, 1806) and Sumburgh Head (Shetland, 1821). When he retired at the age of 70 in 1843 he was succeeded as Engineer to the Northern Lighthouse Board by his eldest son Alan.

The Bell Rock Lighthouse is important for our story because it greatly influenced Alan, and to a lesser extent his two younger brothers David and Thomas, when they risked their lives and reputations building lighthouses on dangerous reefs in stormy seas. It was one thing to construct a lighthouse on the Scottish mainland or an inhabited island with reasonable access and an available labour force, but quite another to work on an isolated rock with no facilities whatsoever. This was the challenge accepted by Alan for his most daring lighthouse, Skerryvore, 12 miles off the Hebridean isle of Tiree, and by David and Thomas when they took on the formidable Muckle Flugga.

Bell Rock forms part of a long and treacherous sandstone reef in the North Sea. It had been a scourge of vessels plying Scotland's east coast for centuries. The reef extends for about 1,500 feet, lurking below the sea surface for much of the time and producing dangerous eddies. Over hundreds of years the reef remained unmarked and dreaded, and by the late 18th century it was exacting a terrible toll on naval and merchant shipping.

From its establishment in 1786 the Northern Lighthouse Board was left in no doubt about the Bell Rock and was under constant pressure to do something about it. Petitions were raised, Parliamentary questions asked, and a hotchpotch of schemes proposed. There were, unsurprisingly, two main problems: the perceived danger and technical difficulty of crowning a wave-washed rock with a lighthouse; and the huge expense. The Commissioners, short of cash, were already fully stretched building and maintaining a

Part of Robert Stevenson's 1824 map of Scotland showing the Bell Rock Lighthouse and Edinburgh on the right, and the Skerryvore rock (awaiting Alan's attention) on the left.

portfolio of shore-based lights and had no stomach for what many of them considered a madcap scheme.

But the Bell Rock menace had already been on Robert Stevenson's mind for many years – and he was determined to do something about it. He was crucially aware of the rock's ability to destroy ships approaching or leaving the Firths of Tay and Forth – the latter hosting Leith, the port of his home city, Edinburgh. He visited the reef in 1800 and, having toyed with the idea of a lighthouse raised on iron pillars, firmed up on plans for a stone tower similar to the famous Eddystone Lighthouse, built by John Smeaton on a wave-washed rock in the English Channel in 1759. Two key features of the Eddystone tower, 68 feet high and weighing 1,000 tons, were its extensive use of stone dovetailing, and a base flared out to lessen the impact of waves.

The Commissioners were eventually persuaded of the need for action on the Bell Rock but dared not entrust the perilous project to Robert on his own. They turned instead to John Rennie, a professional engineer of 44 with an established reputation for building canals, aqueducts, bridges, and docks, and appointed Robert as his deputy. The two men visited the Bell Rock together and, according to Robert:

> They made a favourable landing; and Mr Rennie had only been a short time upon the rock, when he gave his decided opinion upon the practicability of the proposed erection of stone. He had examined the author's designs and models, and afterwards made a Report, in which he coincided with him in recommending to the Board the adoption of a building of stone, on the principles of the Eddystone Light-house.

Rennie could hardly accept the role of Engineer without recommending some ideas of his own, and it is hardly surprising that he suggested modifying Robert's initial proposal, nudging it even closer to Smeaton's Eddystone design. But as the work proceeded Rennie's contribution dwindled to giving advice from a distance – advice that was sometimes ignored – and Robert's blossomed to such an extent that in the public mind as well as that of the Northern Lighthouse Board it became a Stevenson lighthouse. Rennie's descendants continued to argue the toss, but to little effect.

The Bell Rock project cost Robert Stevenson four years of hard labour. A crucial initial decision was to erect a timber 'beacon house' on the rock to act as a warning to shipping and provide temporary accommodation for the workforce. A foundation pit for the lighthouse had to be chiselled out of bare rock by masons using hand tools, even though it was constantly being inundated on flood tides. Carefully shaped stones, dovetailed to fine tolerances, were prepared in a workyard in Arbroath and shipped 11 miles out to the rock in small sailing vessels through dangerous seas. As the tower took shape there were many accidents and occasional deaths, a host of technical problems with stones and cranes, and a near-mutiny by seamen dissatisfied with their beer rations.

Robert's ability to organise men and materials in one of the most dangerous construction projects ever attempted off a European coastline became legendary, and as his lighthouse neared completion the dazzling spectacle attracted many sightseers in small boats. On 1 February 1811 the revolving light commenced its nightly duty, settling the unequal contest between North Sea mariners and the long-dreaded rock. Twenty-seven years later it was his son Alan's destiny to confront the equally deadly Skerryvore reef in the Scottish Hebrides, and crown it with one of the most stunning lighthouses ever built.

Alan was delicate as a child and far from robust as an adult. A lover of literature and poetry, he was an unlikely candidate to follow his formidable and single-minded father into the lighthouse business. He was just four years old when the Bell Rock beamed out over the North Sea, and 17 by the time Robert's account of it was published in 1824. Basically, he lived with it, fascinated and repelled in equal measure at the prospect of entering a profession that, in the middle of the 19th century, placed huge demands on its practitioners.

He grew up in the large and fashionable home, 1 Baxter's Place in Edinburgh's New Town, that Robert built for his family as his fame and income expanded. It was a wonderful place for children, with masses of space and a large garden where Alan and his younger brothers had plenty of mischievous fun. But it was ruled over by a father with an old-fashioned Christian outlook, a superhuman work ethic, and an unbending assumption that his eldest son would join the family business. In 1815, at the age of eight, Alan was dispatched to the local Royal High School and fed the usual diet of classics and natural philosophy. Shy and introspective, he failed to shine in spite of his obvious intelligence, preferring reading and writing to physical activity and giving his father increasing concern. When his education continued at Edinburgh University he remained torn between the arts and sciences, but Robert kept up relentless pressure and eventually received the news he wanted:

The Bell Rock Lighthouse nearing completion. The temporary 'beacon house' on the left provided shelter and accommodation for the workforce. Note the flared-out base of the lighthouse tower, designed to reduce wave impacts.

Dear Father,

I take this opportunity of answering your letter in which you stated a desire that I would apply myself to some business and although I must confess I had a liking for the profession of a soldier, on receipt of your letter I determined to overcome this foolish wish and am happy to say I have succeeded. On further consideration I found in myself a strong desire for literary glory and I picked upon an advocate but there was a want of interest. It was the same way with a clergyman and as I am by no means fond of shop-keeping I determined upon an engineer, especially that all with whom I have spoken on the subject recommend it and as you yourself seemed to point it out as the most fit situation in life I could

```
desire. I only doubt that my talents do not lie that
way, but in hopes that my choice will meet with your
full approbation,

I remain, my dear Father,

Your ever affectionate and grateful son,

Alan Stevenson.
```

Having made up his mind – or, some would say, capitulated – Alan never looked back, and committed a generous slice of heart and soul to the job.

The decision set in motion a programme that mirrored Robert's own introduction to practical engineering with his mentor Thomas Smith more than 30 years before. Alan's seven-year apprenticeship, even broader than his father's, was buttressed by scientific knowledge that eclipsed Robert's more tentative efforts at formal education. The family business was now handling a wide range of engineering projects including roads, bridges, harbours, and railways, so Alan spent summers on projects scattered far from their Edinburgh base, and winters helping his father with a diverse and ever-increasing office workload. He was heavily involved with Robert's later lighthouses and found himself at various times dispatched to bridge works near Dumfries, harbour works in Fife, and river works near Liverpool under the supervision of the great Thomas Telford. He also travelled to Russia, France, and Sweden, mixing engineering with sightseeing and a fascination with foreign lands. And then in 1830 the Northern Lighthouse Board, realising that it had an exceptional young man in its sights, offered him a job as Clerk of Works at a salary of £150 per annum. He was just 23 years old.

Alan's workload, already heavy, increased dramatically. Five more lighthouses including Robert's final gem, Lismore (1833), were built and lit in the next few years, and it was the job of the Clerk of Works to ensure that the works were carried out in the Board's best interests. In view of his history of indifferent health it seems remarkable that he survived such a severe crash course in responsibility for men, money, and materials.

The programme of education and practical experience gave Alan a knowledge of lighthouse engineering unsurpassed by any other man of his age. Unsurprisingly, the Commissioners decided to offer him, in 1838, an additional six guineas a week to take charge of the Skerryvore Lighthouse project. They would not regret their choice.

Robert Stevenson had first landed on the Skerryvore reef, 12 miles off the Isle of Tiree, in 1804. He went back again in 1814, accompanied by Sir Walter Scott and several Commissioners. In the same year Parliament sanctioned the building of a lighthouse, but the Board was in no hurry. Another 20 years was to pass before the pressure to act became irresistible, and then, in 1834, they sent Robert back to Skerryvore to conduct a detailed survey of the reef. This time he was accompanied by Alan and Thomas.

Robert concluded that a lighthouse was not only practicable but promised to be 'much less difficult and expensive than that of the Bell Rock'. This surprising claim glossed over the total lack of facilities on Tiree and the special hazards of Hebridean storms, and probably had more to do with his impatience for action than a realistic appraisal of the difficulties.

In any case the Commissioners decided to inspect Skerryvore themselves in the summer of 1835, and it was perhaps providential that a fire broke out in the steamer's boiler room close to the dreaded rocks, helping clinch the argument for a lighthouse.

Alan devoted six years of his life to Skerryvore. He had no illusions about the magnitude of the task or the special dangers posed by the isolated reef:

> a tract of foul ground, consisting of various small rocks, some always above the level of the sea, others covered at high water, and exposed only at low water, and others, again, constantly under the surface, but on which the sea is often seen to break after heavy gales from the westward. This cluster of rocks extends from Tyree in a south-westerly direction, leaving, however, between that island and the rock called Boinshly, the first of the great Skerryvore cluster, a passage of about five miles in breadth ... This passage is called the passage of Tyree; but it is by no means safe during strong and long continued gales, as the sea which rises between Tyree and Skerryvore, is such that no vessel can live in it.

The passage of Tiree is precisely the stretch of water that Alan and his men would negotiate time and time again as they struggled to Skerryvore and back, transporting every tool and item of equipment, all stores and provisions, and landing over 4,000 tons of granite for the lighthouse tower. The labour involved almost defies our modern imagination.

Nor was the reef itself the only source of difficulty. The isle of Tiree, at a distance of 12 miles, was the nearest land to Skerryvore, and Alan had no alternative but to base his operations there, but it totally lacked the skilled workers and facilities he needed. Basically, it was overpopulated and semi-destitute. There were no wheeled vehicles, agriculture was extremely primitive and the locals lived, for the most part, in dismal cottages. In years of poor harvest they went hungry, and the infamous Highland Clearances were resulting in even worse destitution. It is hardly surprising that the highly educated Alan, brought up in Edinburgh's thriving New Town, found the island uninspiring.

Alan's struggle began in 1838: summer months battling against the elements on Skerryvore, constructing a monumental lighthouse tower that has been called the most graceful in the world; winters back in Edinburgh, planning the next season's work and helping with the family business, watched over by his eagle-eyed father.

He started by constructing a temporary barrack on the rock to house the workforce, identical to his father's design for the Bell Rock, but it was completely destroyed by a winter storm and had to be rebuilt. His granite lighthouse, at 156 feet the tallest ever attempted in Scotland, was to trump Robert's 100-footer on the Bell Rock and weigh twice as much. Alan dispensed with most of the expensive stone dovetailing that his father had used, correctly convinced that weight on its own was sufficient to ensure the tower's strength and stability. He also specified a highly sophisticated revolving light with Fresnel lenses, far more effective than the reflector lamps pioneered by Thomas Smith.

As Skerryvore neared completion in 1843 Robert, on his final voyage of inspection as Engineer to the Northern Lighthouse Board, called to see his son's creation. It is easy

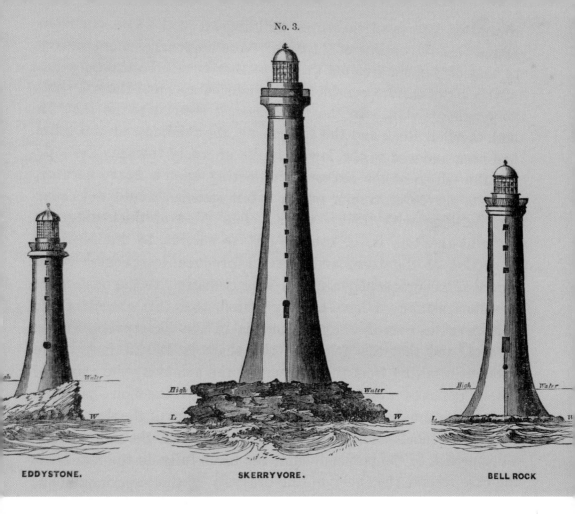

EDDYSTONE.   **SKERRYVORE.**   **BELL ROCK**

Three famous rock lighthouses: Eddystone, Bell Rock, and Skerryvore.

to imagine a heady cocktail of emotions in the two men: a father who had basked in international recognition for his Bell Rock masterpiece for nearly 30 years; and a brilliant but hesitant son, still a lover of poetry and literature, who had just built a tower much higher and arguably more beautiful in an equally impossible location.

Things could never be the same for Alan Stevenson after Skerryvore. Although he was exhausted by his efforts and showed worrying signs of failing health, he applied for the post of Engineer to the Northern Lighthouse Board on the day his father retired, and was appointed in January 1844 at the age of 36. His younger brother Thomas was engaged to put the finishing touches to Skerryvore and complete a dock on Tiree for the lighthouse tender. Meanwhile Alan was thrown in at the deep end, accepting overall responsibility for the Board's lighthouses and undertaking damp and dangerous voyages of inspection around the coast of Scotland. He then started equipping existing lighthouses with the latest lens systems and building new ones. But his health continued its remorseless downward path and he retired from the Northern Lighthouse Board nine years later at the age of 46, suffering from a severe and progressive paralysis.

Family ties: the remarkable Stevensons

47

Fortunately Alan's later years were made more bearable by the love of a wife and children. He had met 21-year-old Margaret Scott Jones at a ball in Anglesey in 1833 and, unsurprisingly for a man who surely needed the love of a young woman, he fell for her. Margaret must have felt the same because she waited 11 years for him. By the time they married he was Engineer to the Board with an astonishing set of achievements to his name including, above all, Skerryvore. Their union produced three daughters and a son Robert – who would become an art critic and teacher – and lasted 21 years. When Alan died in Edinburgh two days before Christmas 1865, the death certificate's medical insight was summarised by a terse 'General paralysis – 8 years'. The Commissioners of the Northern Lighthouse Board recorded their 'deep and abiding regret for the loss of a man ... whose genuine piety, kind heart and high intellect made him beloved'. Few men are granted such an epitaph.

Alan Stevenson's final years can make him seem a sad, even tragic, figure. A man of exceptional intelligence and modesty, a lover of wild nature, a poet and linguist as well as an engineer, he might have been better suited to life as a university don, or, given his profound religious convictions, a country clergyman. But following years of paternal pressure he agreed to subject himself to a profession that was almost guaranteed to test him to destruction. Family ties, in Alan's case, were an extremely mixed blessing.

It had always been Robert Stevenson's ambition – indeed his assumption – that all his sons would become civil engineers. But the next in line, Bob, almost disappeared without trace. As a teenager he showed no interest whatsoever in lighthouses, and very little in any other subject. When he left school his spelling was so hopeless that his horrified father insisted on crash courses in literacy before packing him off to St Andrews University, where he opted for medicine. Somewhat surprisingly he ended up as an army surgeon, but an infectious disease caught in India forced him back to Edinburgh and he died tragically in 1851. He had outlived his disappointed father by a single year.

Next in line for entering the family profession was David, Alan's junior by eight years and destined to take on Muckle Flugga with his brother Thomas. He was far more in Robert's mould – no problems with poetry, delicate health, lack of interest, or indolence, but a boy who seemed cut out from the start to follow in his father's footsteps. Like his brothers he was born in the family home, 1 Baxter's Place in Edinburgh, and sent to the local High School. Robert was delighted with David's steady uncomplicated progress and planned his future meticulously. He was the only son to commit himself wholeheartedly to an engineering career from an early age, and in due course he served an apprenticeship every bit as demanding as Alan's, combining it with academic studies at Edinburgh University between 1831 and 1835. Family ties, in his case, seemed natural and mutually beneficial.

David turned out to be a competent writer who filled vast quantities of notebooks on his travels at home and abroad. His style may be less sensitive than Alan's, but he was far from humourless and would often decorate his neatly written diaries with lively anecdotes and insights. At the tender age of 13 his father took him on what was becoming a family rite of passage – an inspection tour of the Northern Lighthouses – and demanded that he keep a record. Young David's maturing style is already clear from a diary entry he made soon after sailing from Edinburgh in the *Regent* lighthouse vessel:

Our gallant ship being under the command of Captain Soutar. Her cargo consisting of the apparatus for the Lighthouse now building at Cape Wrath. The Regent's tonnage is 141 tons Register though she is at present only half loaded … On our way down the Firth we landed at the Island of Inchkeith and were very much gratified with a view of the Lighthouse. Mr Bonnyman the principal keeper was very attentive in shewing us all his apparatus. He was one of the masons at the building of the Bell Rock Lighthouse in 1809 when he had the misfortune to lose one of his fingers. We here also met with an old Lighthouse Pilot of the name of Noble who had had 20 children. On being asked by my Father how a certain pleasure boat sailed he replied 'Sail Sir, how the Devil could she sail, when the party played at the Cairts on the sabath [sic] day'.

A year later the patriarch took Alan, David, and Thomas on another lighthouse voyage. It was David's first experience of Orkney and Shetland, complete with a six-day storm that seriously interrupted the itinerary but seems to have left his stomach undisturbed. He can hardly have imagined that 25 years later he would travel once again in foul weather to the Northern Isles and encounter the awesome Muckle Flugga.

When David left school Robert arranged some initial work experience with James Scott, a millwright in the town of Cupar, Fife. Uncomfortably lodged in the house of 'a respectable widow', fortified by sausages and Finnan haddock smoked over green wood and peat, the 14-year-old was clearly homesick and had a headache 'almost every day'. The pains eased when Scott sent him to help install new machinery at a flax-spinning mill just 8 miles from Edinburgh, allowing him to walk home at weekends. But he had two narrow escapes from death, one thanks to some careless shooters engaged in target practice, the other while trying to reach an upper room in the mill building by clambering up its giant water wheel which, to the huge consternation of onlookers, began to rotate.

David was much tougher physically than Alan and it stood him in good stead during a formidable apprenticeship. He spent time in the office learning the family business and was dispatched to projects in Scotland, England, and Ireland, covering bridges, harbours, rivers, roads, tunnels, railways and, last but not least, lighthouses. He was expected to help foremen with organisation and masons with heavy manual work, often enduring uncomfortable nights in dismal lodgings followed by rain-soaked days in remote locations. He occasionally wrote to his mother confessing loneliness, but dared not mention it to a father who was tone deaf to any expression of personal weakness.

One of David's summer tasks was to prove a hard lesson in isolation. The Mull of Kintyre Lighthouse in the southwest of Scotland, originally built by Thomas Smith in 1788 and rebuilt by Robert in the 1820s, still lacked a decent access road from Campbeltown, many miles away across rough moorland. Perched three quarters of the way down a vertiginous headland, the lighthouse had never been approachable by sea so everything had to be brought on horseback. David was given the task of upgrading the track, building bridges, avoiding bogs and pitfalls. Today, a notice beside the single-track road, just before its precipitous descent to the lighthouse, congratulates the traveller on 'safely negotiating one of Scotland's most exciting roads'.

By the time David's apprenticeship ended in 1835 he was well equipped to deliver the first of several papers to the Royal Scottish Society of Arts, founded 14 years previously 'for the Encouragement of the Useful Arts in Scotland'. His early contact with the Society encouraged its president, the Duke of Buccleuch, Scottish land magnate and Conservative politician, to offer him an appointment as resident engineer in charge of new harbour works at Granton, Edinburgh. This first job was conveniently close to home and paid a welcome £150 per annum, but it was to last less than two years because professional disagreements more or less forced David's resignation. At this point Robert was keen to have him back in the family business, but the itchy feet of a 22-year-old, recently engaged but not yet married, suggested something more adventurous.

David opted for America and sailed for New York in March 1837. He was lucky to arrive because his ship, the *Sheffield*:

> was close beset by field ice off the banks of Newfoundland for about 16 hours which, as appeared when she was docked in New York, carried off her false keel and stripped away every square foot of copper off her bottom. Our Captain who had made more than 100 voyages between Liverpool and New York and had never touched ice before was in great fear for his ship.

The young engineer visited many cities and sites in America and Canada before returning via France, Switzerland, Germany and the Netherlands. Shortly afterwards he wrote his influential *Sketch of the Civil Engineering of North America* which, among other things, introduced new designs of fast steam vessels with fine lines into Britain.

David was now back in Edinburgh and, in May 1838, he and Alan joined their 66-year-old father as partners in the family firm, renamed Robert Stevenson and Sons. Alan had just started his all-consuming six-year commitment to Skerryvore, so David took on the responsibility for general management of the firm's business including many harbour, river, and canal projects, a role he continued for the next 43 years. He became an acknowledged expert on tidal flows in estuaries and even advised on salmon fishing disputes in fast-flowing Scottish rivers. As the railway boom gathered pace, he was asked to conduct courts of enquiry into railway projects. His work continued to diversify and expand, at home and abroad, and in 1844 he became a fellow of the Royal Society of Edinburgh and a member of the Institution of Civil Engineers.

When Alan retired due to ill health in 1853 the Northern Lighthouse Board appointed David as its Engineer, propelling him firmly back into lighthouse engineering. It was a second baptism, if not by fire then certainly by water, because the next year found him sailing to Shetland and inspecting the dizzy heights of Muckle Flugga. In 1855 the Commissioners agreed, at David's repeated request, to offer his younger brother Thomas a joint appointment to share the heavy workload. Over the next 30 years the pair went on to design and build 29 new lighthouses around the coasts of Scotland, including four on

Family ties: Alan, David, and Thomas Stevenson with their wives and children in 1860. The ailing Alan, aged 53 and by now head of the family, sits in the centre with Margaret and their son Robert, aged 13, behind him. On the right is David, aged 45, flanked by a nanny, daughters and wife Elizabeth. Standing at the front are their two young sons, David A. and Charles. Centre-left at the back, Thomas, aged 42, stands with wife Maggie and their son Robert Louis, aged 9. (© Leslie and Paxton, 1999).

our list: Out Skerries (Shetland, 1854); Bressay (Shetland, 1858); Muckle Flugga (Shetland, 1858); and Auskerry (Orkney, 1866).

In 1840 David married his childhood sweetheart Elizabeth Mackay, daughter of a goldsmith. The Mackay family lived near the Stevensons in Edinburgh and the two had played together as children. By the ages of 16 and 14 they were busy carving their initials on a tree beside the River Forth at Stirling, and engagement followed shortly before David started working for the Duke of Buccleuch at Granton. The marriage produced eight children including David Alan (David A.) and Charles. They, in turn, would continue the family's engineering tradition and its unique association with the Northern Lighthouse Board.

We may leave David Stevenson's story for the time being and introduce Thomas, known in the family as Tom, the fourth and youngest son of Robert and Jean Stevenson. Three years David's junior, he was to become a famous lighthouse engineer in his own right.

Like his brothers, Tom was born in the family home, 1 Baxter's Place in Edinburgh's New Town. The severe discipline of a Victorian preparatory school gave him a lifelong distrust of formal education and when he followed his brothers to the local high school he was described as a reluctant pupil 'wanting in arithmetic'. Instead he put his overt energies into learning Latin and his covert ones into collecting old books, writing stories, and engaging in flights of fancy. There were already plenty of signs that his entry into the civil engineering profession, if it happened at all, would be far less straightforward than David's.

His father, remembering reticent Alan and troublesome Bob, decided to shunt his youngest son into one of the few areas that seemed to engage him. So on leaving school Tom entered the printing firm of one of Robert's friends and was introduced to the mysteries of typography. A fleeting interest in bookselling and publishing followed, but boredom soon set in and drove him to request a formal apprenticeship in the family firm. By the age of 17 he was installed in his father's Edinburgh office and enrolled at Edinburgh University.

Young Tom was soon making sketches and collecting survey data for the firm's coastal works. His unquenched literary ambitions, plus a tendency to go off at tangents, produced a rather casual attitude towards the family business compared with his two older brothers. During his apprenticeship he found plenty of time to write his own stories and received a written demand from Robert to 'give up such nonsense and mind your business'. Whether or not he obeyed is unclear, but it was impossible for a Stevenson apprentice to escape the father's insistent attention. He was put through a programme hardly less severe than David's, and by the age of 21 had gained wide experience in harbour design, river improvement and lighthouse construction, backed up by classes at Edinburgh University.

The importance of reliable and accurate measurements was impressed on Tom by his father and would remain with him throughout a long working life. He developed an instinctive understanding of natural phenomena including waves, winds and tides, and devised novel instruments for measuring them. Coupled with his growing scientific awareness was a romantic, other-worldly, temperament that made him difficult to work with, and he would spend countless hours on observations that had little to do with the immediate needs of the Stevenson business. But Robert allowed his youngest son considerable leeway, no doubt relieved to have steered him in more or less the right direction. Family ties, in Tom's case, proved rather elastic.

By 1842 the 24-year-old was busy testing his own design of 'marine dynamometer' on rocks beside the Little Ross Lighthouse near Kirkcudbright, in what was probably the first attempt to measure wave pressures directly. The device was subsequently used at Skerryvore and the Bell Rock, indicating the enormous forces that attacked the two lighthouses, and he presented his findings to the Royal Society of Edinburgh in 1848. In the early 1850s he switched attention to measuring wave heights at various locations around the Scottish coast, concluding that they increased roughly in proportion to the square root of the distance from the windward shore – an approximation used by marine engineers for over a century. As the years went by his painstaking observations made him a world expert on the effects of waves and tides on man-made structures. His book on the design and construction of harbours was published in 1864, the year in which he became a member of the Institution of Civil Engineers.

In 1846 the 74-year-old Robert Stevenson released his grip on the family firm and Tom joined his two brothers as a partner. With David as principal office manager and Alan heavily committed to his role as Engineer to the Northern Lighthouse Board, Tom began a long and fruitful career biased towards what we would now call R&D. Although he certainly contributed to the family's money-making activities and, from 1855 to 1887, collaborated first with David and finally with his nephew David A. as joint Engineer to the Board, he never lost his love of original investigation. New fields, including meteorology, were pursued in a highly individualistic way. A curious combination of intuitive scientist, hesitant career engineer, romantic and eccentric made Tom a more complex and volatile character than either Robert or David.

Tom's partnership in the family business gave him real money to play with, and it was time to think of marriage. He had met the 18-year-old love of his life on a railway journey to Glasgow and proposed to her during a walk on the Pentland Hills. Tall, elegant Margaret ('Maggie') Balfour was the youngest daughter of the Reverend Lewis Balfour, minister of the parish church of Colinton, then a village outside Edinburgh. They were married in August 1848 and moved into a small city house at 8 Howard Place, Edinburgh, later to become something of a literary shrine because their only son Robert Louis Stevenson was born there in 1850. Maggie's bridesmaid visited them soon afterwards and was fascinated by what she discovered:

> It was an intense interest for me to watch the development of my girl friend into a wife and mother and to study the character of her grave and scientific husband. He delighted in her livelier spirits, for left to himself, life was 'full of sairiousness' to him; and had it not been for his strong sense of humour, which was a striking trait in his character, the Calvinism in which he had been brought up would have left its gloomy mark upon him.

In August of that same year, 1850, three months before Robert Louis was born, Robert Stevenson passed away. By then Tom, the maverick son who had flirted with Latin, literature, and typography before settling into a Stevenson career, had made good. But Robert could hardly have guessed that he would add to his other accomplishments by becoming a world expert on lighthouse optics.

Alan and Tom both realised that one of the last great challenges of Victorian lighthouse engineering was to transform expensive fuel oil into a finely focused light beam as efficiently as possible. Alan, who had met and befriended the Fresnel brothers, French pioneers of glass lenses for lighthouses, crowned his Skerryvore tower with the most sophisticated system ever used in Britain. As Engineer to the Northern Lighthouse Board he went on to substitute lens systems for old reflector lamps in existing lighthouses, an early example being one on our list – Thomas Smith's classic on the Pentland Skerries between John o' Groats and Orkney.

As Alan's health deteriorated, Tom increasingly took up the challenge. In March of that memorable year, 1850, he took his first step towards international fame by submitting a paper to the Royal Scottish Society of Arts on his new 'holophotal system'. This used a combination of reflectors, prisms and a Fresnel lens to collect and concentrate the entire sphere of a lamp's diverging rays and direct them towards the horizon. The first holophotal light was installed at Peterhead in 1849 and followed by a larger-scale version at North

Ronaldsay, Orkney in 1853. Tom's crowning achievement, first employed at Isle Ornsay Lighthouse on Skye in 1857, was his 'azimuthal condensing system' which concentrated the available light in the directions most important for navigation. The work became widely known and appreciated through his classic 1859 work, *Lighthouse Illumination*.

There was a slight hiatus in Tom's published work in the early 1860s because Maggie and young Robert Louis were showing worrying signs of chronic ill-health. She was 'delicate' and often stayed in bed until noon; their child caught all the Victorian ailments and was hard hit by them. Family life was increasingly disrupted and they moved house in 1853 and again in 1857 largely for medical reasons. Mother and son began to travel south in summer to recuperate from the Scottish winter and in 1863 the whole family spent five months abroad. Tom was completely devoted to Maggie and considered it his Christian duty to support her and Robert Louis in every way possible.

Apart from family problems, the 1860s landed Tom with a monumental headache in the form of a breakwater he and David were building at Wick on the north-east coast of Scotland – a headache later described by Robert Louis as the chief disaster of his father's life. The British Fisheries Society had decided that an improved 'harbour of refuge' was required along that unforgiving coast and construction started in 1863. Five years later the breakwater had been built 1,000 feet out into Wick Bay, ending in water 30 feet deep. But David and Tom failed to anticipate what they were up against and major storm damage occurred in 1870, 1872, and especially 1877 when 2,600 tons of stonework were carried away by the sea. Repair after repair proved fruitless and the breakwater was eventually abandoned as a costly failure.

The Wick harbour project was a rare setback in the annals of Stevenson engineering and the brothers were undoubtedly hurt by it. But Tom, in particular, must have been comforted by the distractions of his new passion, lighthouse optics, an altogether gentler affair. *Lighthouse Construction and Illumination*, expanded and updated from his earlier book, was published in 1881.

Fortunately another of Tom's and David's joint endeavours, illuminating the eastern coastlines of Orkney and Shetland with four superb lighthouses, had already been crowned with success, and nowhere more so than on Muckle Flugga, the brothers' most formidable challenge. By the time that work started in the 1850s the Northern Lighthouse Board's portfolio included 27 major lighthouses, so they had plenty of background to draw on. Above all, they gained inspiration from their father's Bell Rock and Alan's Skerryvore – not so much for the details of design and construction as for the extraordinary determination the Stevenson family had already shown in placing lights on Scotland's offshore rocks.

4 EYE WITNESS: SIR WALTER SCOTT

The Stevenson story is intertwined with the economic and social conditions in the Scottish Highlands and Islands where so many of their lighthouses were built. Over the years the family built up a wealth of experience, recorded for posterity in technical notes, diaries, and workbooks, and discussed by father and sons in lively conversation. Fortunately for us, their story was further illuminated by two internationally famous authors, Sir Walter Scott (1771–1832), and Robert Louis Stevenson (1850–94).

Walter Scott, whose Edinburgh monument is the tallest in the world ever dedicated to a writer, has left us an eye-witness account of Robert Stevenson's inspection of the Scottish lights in 1814. For an insight into 19th-century conditions around the coasts of Scotland, including the Northern Isles, we could hardly be in better company. The annual inspection was a firm fixture in the Northern Lighthouse Board's schedule and would, in due course, try and test Alan, David, and Thomas.

On 29 July 1814 Scott, already a famous poet but not yet a baronet, sailed from Leith, the port of Edinburgh, as a guest aboard the Northern Lighthouse Board's yacht *Pharos*. Among the passengers were several Commissioners, two further guests, and Robert Stevenson. The voyage of inspection would take them as far north as Orkney and Shetland before returning to Glasgow via the Pentland Firth, Cape Wrath, and the Hebridean islands.

Just three weeks before departure Scott had seen *Waverley,* his first historical novel, published in Edinburgh to huge critical acclaim. The initial print run of 1,000 copies was sold out in two days. He had decided to keep his name off the book, swayed by the contemporary view that novel writing was beneath the dignity of a famous poet, but almost every reviewer guessed his identity. Jane Austen, whose *Pride and Prejudice* had hit the bookshops the previous year, recognised his hand and was not best pleased by the competition:

> Walter Scott has no business to write novels, especially good ones – it is not fair. He has Fame and Profit enough as a Poet, and should not be taking the bread out of other people's mouths – I do not like him, and do not mean to like Waverley if I can help it – but fear I must.

Scott was probably relieved to swap Edinburgh's febrile literary atmosphere for the tossing of a lighthouse yacht. He was busy on a new narrative poem, *The Lord of the Isles,* and needed to witness as much Highland scenery, culture, and local colour as possible.

Walter Scott and his Edinburgh monument (Wikipedia).

It was actually a brave decision because the 43-year-old had never fully recovered from the polio that rendered him lame as a young child. Six weeks on a small sailing vessel was unlikely to make a restful break and, although Napoleon had been temporarily confined to Elba, the United States was still at war with Britain and its privateers were busy ambushing vessels in Scottish waters.

Voyage of the Pharos, Scott's diary of the adventure, is rich in history, social conditions, and landscape. As a romantic writer he was hardly best placed to comment on lighthouse engineering, but he clearly developed great admiration for Robert Stevenson. Every now and again we get a delicious glimpse of the literary giant's attitude towards the professional engineer, whom he acknowledged as 'the official chief of the expedition ... a most gentlemanlike and modest man, and well known by his scientific skill'.

One day out of Leith, the *Pharos* dropped anchor off the Bell Rock. Scott had read all about the iconic lighthouse, lit three years before, but was still mesmerised by the actual experience:

> Waked at six by the steward: summoned to visit the Bell Rock, where the beacon is well worthy attention. Its dimensions are well known; but no description can give the idea of this slight, solitary, round tower, trembling amid the billows, and fifteen miles from Arbroath, the nearest shore. The fitting up within is not only handsome, but elegant ... you enter by a ladder of rope, with wooden steps, about

The port of Leith, Edinburgh, in 1818, by William Daniell, (NLS).

thirty feet from the bottom, where the mason-work ceases to be solid, and admits of round apartments. The lowest is a storehouse for the people's provisions, water, etc.; above that a storehouse for the lights, of oil, etc.; then the kitchen of the people, three in number; then their sleeping chamber; then the saloon or parlour, a neat little room; above all, the lighthouse; all communicating by oaken ladders, with brass rails, most handsomely and conveniently executed. Breakfasted in the parlour.

The meal was not entirely carefree because he was coaxed into contributing to the visitors' book. The poem *Pharos Loquitur* ('The Lighthouse Speaks') sprang from his pen:

> Far in the bosom of the deep,
> O'er these wild shelves my watch I keep;
> A ruddy gem of changeful light,
> Bound on the dusky brow of night,
> The Seaman bids my lustre hail,
> And scorns to strike his timorous sail.

Bell Rock Lighthouse (Geograph/Colin Wheatley); and Arbroath signal tower (Wikipedia).

All the passengers, including Robert Stevenson, were sick as the vessel ploughed through rough seas to Arbroath, but they pulled themselves together and inspected the lighthouse signal tower and the apartments built for keepers' families before sailing again in the evening.

Captain Wilson now showed what the *Pharos* and his crew could achieve. After a brief call at Girdle Ness where 'the magistrates of Aberdeen wish to have a fort and beacon light', an excursion ashore to explore rock formations near Peterhead, and an inspection of the Kinnaird Head Lighthouse at Fraserburgh by Robert and the Commissioners, they 'stretched for Shetland'. Just three days after leaving Arbroath:

> we begin to think we have passed the Fair Isle, lying between Shetland and Orkney, at which it was our intention to have touched. In short, like one of Sinbad's adventures, we have run on till neither captain nor pilot know exactly where we are. The breeze increases – weather may be called rough; worse and worse after we are in our berths, nothing but booming, trampling, and whizzing of waves about our ears, and ever and anon, as we fall asleep, our ribs come in contact with those of the vessel ...

The following morning there was still no sight of land, and Scott mused that the Sheriff of Shetland should 'issue a warrant against his territories, which seem to fly from us'. Fair Isle was living up to its reputation as the most isolated inhabited island in the British Isles, surrounded by restless seas and all too easily missed in the days of sail. It would have to wait another 78 years for its Stevenson lighthouses. After this worrying episode the captain was relieved to reach Shetland's capital, Lerwick, in the late evening of 2 August.

At the time of the voyage there was only one lighthouse along the eastern coastlines of the Northern Isles – Start Point, Orkney, which had been completed by Robert Stevenson eight years before. So the voyage of inspection, after clearing the Scottish mainland, had very little to do further north. Indeed we might wonder why it included Shetland at all. The answer seems to lie in two parts: one of the passengers was William Erskine, Sheriff of Orkney and Shetland who was also, *ex officio,* a Commissioner; and another was the Reverend Turnbull, minister of Tingwall in Shetland. Both had been promised a passage from Leith to Lerwick. More interesting from our point of view is that the whole question of lighthouses for Shetland was already under discussion and Robert Stevenson needed to spy out the land.

Walter Scott spent a week in and around Shetland and it fascinated him. An Edinburgh man, a lawyer and member of the Tory establishment as well as a famous poet, he now found himself visiting an island chain with starkly unfamiliar social and geographical conditions. He was puzzled by many aspects of Shetland life including its contorted system of land tenure, primitive farming, and lack of wheeled vehicles. But he was always eager to listen and learn. As a youngster he had spent long periods convalescing from polio on his grandparents' farm in the Scottish Borders, where he began a lifelong love affair with the culture and folklore of wild Scotland. He would become its great historic novelist, champion of all things highland and tartan, and smoother of long-held antipathies arising from the Jacobite rebellion of 1745. His attitude towards the Highlands and Islands was basically one of empathy.

A glimpse of modern Lerwick (Geograph/Rob Farrow).

However Lerwick, in spite of its superb natural harbour, failed to enchant him:

> a poor-looking place, the streets flagged instead of being causewayed, for there are no wheel-carriages. The streets full of drunken riotous sailors, from the whale-vessels. It seems these ships take about 1000 sailors from Zetland every year, and return them as they come back from the fishery. Each sailor may gain from £20 to £30 … and make a point of treating English messmates, who get drunk of course, and are very riotous. The Zetlanders themselves do not get drunk, but go straight home to their houses, and reserve their hilarity for the winter season, when they spend their wages in dancing and drinking.

He certainly made good use of his time on Shetland. On excursions away from the capital he marvelled at the 'tremendously sublime' cliff scenery of Bressay and Noss, rode over to Tingwall on a Shetland pony to visit the Reverend Turnbull in his manse, and explored ancient ruins. He was constantly inquisitive about Shetland life and folklore, including the 'numerous and potent' superstitions of the islanders:

> The dwarfs are the prime agents in the machinery of Norwegian superstition. The trows do not differ from the fairies of the Lowlands, or Sighean of the Highlanders. They steal children, dwell within the interior of green hills, and often carry mortals into their recesses. Sometimes, when a person becomes melancholy and low spirited, the trows are supposed to have stolen the real being, and left a moving phantom to represent him. Sometimes they are said to steal only the heart – like Lancashire witches. There are cures in each case.
>
> A worse and most horrid opinion prevails, or did prevail, among the fishers – namely, that he who saves a drowning man will receive at his hands some deep wrong or injury. Several instances were quoted today in company, in which the utmost violence had been found necessary to compel the fishers to violate this inhuman prejudice.

A day before leaving Shetland, Scott walked with two companions to a vantage point above the southern end of Bressay Sound, close to the spot where almost half a century later Robert Stevenson's sons David and Thomas would build the Bressay Lighthouse. The view to the south was delightful – 'a succession of capes, headlands, and islands, as far as the cape called Sumburgh Head, which is the furthest point of Zetland in that direction'.

The final evening in Shetland was spent in impressive company:

> We are now to dress for dinner with the Notables of Lerwick, who give us an entertainment in the Town Hall. Oho! … Just as we were going to dinner, the yacht appeared, and Mr Stevenson landed. He gives a

The Broch of Mousa, outside and inside (Geograph/Rob Farrow).

most favourable account of the isles to the northward, particularly Unst … Are hospitably received and entertained by the Lerwick gentlemen. They are a quick intelligent race – chiefly Scottish birth, as appears from their names Mowat, Gifford, Scott, and so forth. These are the chief proprietors. The Norwegian or Danish surnames, though of course the more ancient, belong, with some exceptions, to the lower ranks.

It is clear that Robert Stevenson had stolen away for the day to inspect Shetland's northern outposts and, since he got as far as Unst, he may well have seen Muckle Flugga. Whether he considered it suitable for a lighthouse is unclear.

The *Pharos* sailed from Lerwick early the next morning, 9 August, and, after dropping anchor to allow Scott and Stevenson to inspect the famous Broch of Mousa, beat south to Sumburgh Head in worsening weather. Huge waves were crashing against the broken cliffs, the notorious tidal race known as the Sumburgh Roost ('the head onto the thunderous noise' in old Norse) was in vicious mood, and Captain Wilson almost despaired of finding a safe anchorage.

Robert Stevenson had come to survey the headland on which he would build Shetland's first lighthouse, but Scott's priorities were literary and he decided to explore it on his own. The cliffs were formed of unstable rock and he sent a huge boulder down from the highest crag, watching it shatter and descend into the ocean like a shower of shrapnel. The dramatic scenery suggested a poem to the 'Genius of Sumburgh Head', but he opted for a more physical celebration by sliding down a steep green slope on his bottom. On regaining the *Pharos* he found everything 'made snug' – a clear warning that the passengers were in for a rough night. And, sure enough, by next morning:

> The omen was but too true – a terrible combustion on board, among plates, dishes, glasses, writing-desks, etc. etc.; not a wink of sleep. We weigh and stand out into that delightful current called Sumburgh-rost or rust. This tide certainly owes us a grudge, for it drove us to the eastward about thirty miles on the night of the first (of August), and occasioned our missing the Fair Isle, and now it has caught us on our return. All the landsmen sicker than sick, and our Viceroy, Stevenson, qualmish … this morning I have headache and nausea … he must have a stouter heart than mine who can contemplate without horror the situation of a vessel of an inferior description caught among the these headlands and reefs of rocks, in the long and dark winter nights of these regions. Accordingly, wrecks are frequent. It is proposed to have a light on Sumburgh-head, which is the first land made by vessels coming from the eastward.

Sumburgh Head in gentle weather, crowned by Robert Stevenson's 1821 lighthouse (Geograph/Julian Paren).

Poet and engineer both left Shetland convinced that a lighthouse was sorely needed, not only to guide ships on passage, but to prevent them from dashing themselves to pieces around the headland. Robert Stevenson would complete it seven years later, and his sons David and Thomas salute it on their voyages to and from Muckle Flugga in the 1850s.

Captain Wilson, having missed Fair Isle on the way out, was determined to make landfall on the return; and sure enough, by ten o'clock the next morning one of the local boats was coming out to greet them:

> a strange-looking thing without an entire plank in it, excepting one on each side, upon the strength of which the whole depends, the rest being patched and joined. This trumpery skiff the men manage with the most astonishing dexterity, and row with remarkable speed; they have two banks, that is, two rowers on each bench, and use very short paddles. The wildness of their appearance, with long elf-locks, striped worsted caps, and shoes of raw hide – the fragility of their boat – and their extreme curiosity about us and our cutter, give them a title to be distinguished as natives.

The 250 islanders, who lived and married entirely among themselves, grew barley, oats, and potatoes, and kept warm with peat cut from mossy land on the east side. The all-important fish catches were the property of the tacksman, Mr Strong, a landholder of intermediate status in Highland society who was admired by the sub-tenants for his generosity. Although he sent most of the fish for sale in Lerwick or Kirkwall, there was plenty to spare and the islanders could afford to be choosy – 'skate they will not touch; dog fish they say is only food for Orkney-men'. A favourite but even more dangerous occupation than fishing was fowling – risking their necks to catch young sea birds on the vertiginous cliffs. Meanwhile the women looked after their families and, when time allowed, knitted stockings, night-caps, and 'similar trifles' to barter with passing ships. Unfortunately the current state of war with America prevented them swapping stockings or a dozen eggs for a much-prized bottle of transatlantic brandy.

Scott found the inhabitants 'a good-looking race, more like Zetlanders than Orkney-men'. He judged them primitive and simple, but sober, good-humoured, and friendly. He went off to investigate some of Fair Isle's dramatic cliff scenery and dangled his legs over a precipice:

> but I could not get free of two or three well-meaning islanders who held me fast by the skirts all the time – for it must be conceived, that our numbers and appointments had drawn out the whole population to admire and attend us. After we separated, each, like the nucleus of a comet, had his own distinct train of attendants.

Complimentary though he was about much of the island and its inhabitants, he could not come to terms with their domestic arrangements. Much of his life had been spent in a

The southern end of Fair Isle, showing one of its lighthouses (photo: Tommy Hyndman).

fashionable family home in Edinburgh, and he was overwhelmed by the contrast with Fair Isle's 'capital town':

> a wretched assemblage of the basest huts, dirty without, and still dirtier within; pigs, fowls, cows, men, women, and children, all living promiscuously under the same roof, and in the same room – the brood sow making (among the more opulent) a distinguished inhabitant of the mansion. The compost, a liquid mass of utter abomination, is kept in a square pond of seven feet deep; when I censured it, they allowed it might be dangerous to the bairns; but appeared unconscious of any other objection. I cannot wonder that they want meal, for assuredly they waste it. A great bowie or wooden vessel of porridge is made in the morning; a child comes and sups a few spoonfuls; then Mrs Sow takes her share; then the rest of the children or the parents, and all at pleasure; then come the poultry when the mess is more cool; the rest is flung upon the dunghill – and the goodwife wonders and complains when she wants meal in winter.

Yet in spite of the squalor, the 'natives' were long-lived. It may have been the sea air and fish diet; or perhaps the schoolmaster's reading of scripture in the church each Sunday – assuming he was sober – bolstered by summer visits from the minister of Dunrossness in Shetland, who married lovers and sprinkled babies with holy water. We may wonder how all this mixed with island superstitions, probably even more 'numerous and potent' than those of Shetland.

Robert Stevenson also did his bit to explore Fair Isle, but had his own agenda. He went off with one of the Commissioners to inspect the remains of a primitive Danish light on Ward Hill, the island's highest point, and returned with some specimens of copper ore. He could hardly have guessed that Fair Isle would eventually get two fine lighthouses, but at its furthest ends, and built by two grandsons he would never see.

Scott ends his account of Fair Isle with a reflection on the year 1588, the year in which the Spanish Armada, having encountered Sir Francis Drake, attempted to flee home via the North Sea and the treacherous waters around Orkney and Shetland. There were multiple wrecks, mainly on the west coast of Ireland, but one of the Spanish flagships, *El Gran Grifón,* got no further than Fair Isle:

> In this place, and perhaps in the very cottage now inhabited by Mr Strong, the Duke of Medina Sidonia, Commander-in-Chief of the Invincible Armada, wintered, after losing his vessel to the eastward of the island. It was not till he had spent some weeks in this miserable abode, that he got off to Norway. Independently of the moral consideration, that, from the pitch of power in which he stood a few days before, the proudest peer of the proudest nation in Europe found himself dependent on the jealous and scanty charity of these secluded islanders, it is scarce possible not to reflect with compassion on the change of situation from the palaces of Estramadura to the hamlet of the Fair Isle.

The *Pharos* spent a single day anchored off Fair Isle and was away by evening. The visit made a huge impression on the islanders, fortified by gifts of whisky and tobacco and a donation for the purchase of staple foodstuffs. They raised flags on their signal-post as the visitors departed and were answered from the vessel by hoisted colours and a three-gun salute that 'echoed from a thousand caves'.

After a sound sleep the passengers awoke to find the yacht anchored off Sanday, one of Orkney's largest islands. They had sailed 20 miles across the ocean, bypassing North Ronaldsay which only had an unlit masonry tower to act as a warning to shipping. But Sanday boasted the fine lighthouse at Start Point, built eight years earlier by Robert Stevenson and the first in Scotland to be equipped with a revolving light. He and the Commissioners had come to inspect it, and Scott was suitably impressed:

> A lighthouse has been erected lately upon the best construction. Landed and surveyed it. All in excellent order, and the establishment of the keepers in the same style of comfort and respectability as elsewhere, far better than the house of the master of the Fair Isle, and rivalling my own baronial mansion of Abbotsford. Go to the top of the tower and survey the island, which, as the name implies, is level, flat, and sandy, quite the reverse of those in Zetland: it is intersected by creeks and small lakes, and, though it abounds with shell marle, seems barren.

Sanday from the air (Geograph/Julian Paren); and Robert Stevenson's lighthouse at Start Point (NLB).

Low-lying Sanday had long been notorious for wrecks. In misty conditions its flatness made it almost invisible from the sea, and ships could be driven ashore without warning. The new lighthouse was undoubtedly a blessing to mariners, but Scott soon learned that it was viewed with suspicion by the islanders, who valued any flotsam and jetsam washed up on the shoreline. Wood was particularly prized on a windswept island bereft of trees, and even ripped canvas had its uses:

> Mr Stevenson happened to observe that the boat of a Sanda farmer had bad sails. "If it had been His (i.e. God's) will that you hadna built sae many lighthouses here about" answered the Orcadian, with great composure, "I would have had new sails last winter". Thus do they talk and think upon these subjects … I fear the poor mariner has little chance of any very anxious attempt to assist him.

The *Pharos* struggled away from Sanday against high winds and a boisterous tide that reminded Scott of the Sumburgh Roost and made him fear for his 'roast and boiled'. Just as upsetting was the spectacle of 265 whales driven ashore by local boats and awaiting their fate from long whaling knives. He was glad to escape among the neighbouring islands, low and green without a cliff in sight, and relieved when they found reasonable shelter in Lingholm Bay off Stronsay. After all the buffeting the passengers looked forward to their dinner aboard, but an 'unlucky sea' had found its way into the galley, and the planned soup, cod, haddock and curry had 'all gone to the devil'. The unlucky cook was expected to conjure up alternatives.

On 12 August, three days out of Lerwick, they reached Kirkwall, Orkney's capital. Scott was principally interested in huge old St Magnus Cathedral, which had escaped the 'blind fury' of the Reformation and was still in good order. It made a fine spectacle from the sea, but the town turned out to be a 'poor and dirty' place, especially near the harbour. The next day he explored the country around Kirkwall, noting the use of oxen and ponies, and the abundance of grouse. He found Orkney's soil and air more genial than Shetland's, and enjoyed the sight of vegetables growing well in the gardens. However attempts to raise trees in the shelter of walls seemed fruitless, and even brushwood had to be imported – a local by the name of Malcolm Laing had ordered a bundle of 'this trash' to be shipped 200 miles from Arbroath to help support his peas. After a day of mixed exploration Robert Stevenson and the other visitors were presented with the freedom of the borough by local worthies before embarking in readiness for an early departure on the morning tide of 14 August.

The pharological interest of Scott's diary now increases again, for the next task was to inspect the Pentland Skerries Lighthouse. After that they would pick up a passenger at Stromness, Orkney's second borough, and sail west towards Cape Wrath and the Hebrides.

It was not as easy as it sounds. Exceptional seamanship was required to navigate among Orkney's maze of islands in fickle weather, especially in a sailing boat without engine, radio, radar, depth sounder or modern charts. The *Pharos* was by no means on a

St Magnus Cathedral, Kirkwall (Wikipedia/Stevekeiretsu).

pleasure trip; her captain had a schedule to meet and his passengers included the Northern Lighthouse Board's Engineer, several Commissioners who were also Sheriffs of the realm, and Scotland's most famous living poet. Sailing in darkness, unless on open ocean, was extremely dangerous and a local port or sheltered bay had to be found each evening. Time and again Mr Wilson must have been at his wits' end as plans were adjusted to take account of the notorious tidal waters – 'no boatman or sailor in Orkney thinks of the wind in comparison of the tides and currents'.

The accompanying historic map of the Orkney Islands, made long before the Churchill Barriers were built to prevent enemy submarines entering Scapa Flow in World War II, is marked with the approximate course of *Pharos* between 11 August 1814, when she reached Orkney from Fair Isle, and 17 August, when she departed for Cape Wrath. To summarise:

- 11 August: arrived Sunday for inspection of Start Point Lighthouse; anchored for the night off Stronsay (distance covered about 20 miles).
- 12 August: sailed from Stronsay to Kirkwall (about 20 miles).
- 13 August: moored in Kirkwall harbour.
- 14 August: sailed from Kirkwall about 4 a.m., reached Scapa Flow about 10 a.m., anchored briefly in Widewall Bay; abandoned plan to inspect Pentland Skerries Lighthouse because of extreme tides; attempted to visit Thurso on the north coast of mainland Scotland, but turned back as the wind dropped; anchored overnight in Long Hope Bay, Orkney (about 60 miles).
- 15 August: sailed from Long Hope to Muckle Skerry for inspection of Pentland Skerries Lighthouse; returned to Long Hope and continued to Stromness Bay via the west side of Scapa Flow (about 40 miles).
- 16 August: remained in Stromness Bay.
- 17 August: sailed out of Hoy Sound in the evening, westward-bound (about 10 miles).

So in five days of sailing the *Pharos* logged about 150 miles in treacherous waters, not including countless tacks back and forth in contrary winds. Robert Stevenson took the whole thing in his stride; and even Scott and his companions, most of whom had been as sick as dogs en route from Leith to Lerwick, were beginning to feel like seasoned sailors.

After they left Kirkwall, Scott continued his shrewd, and often amusing, commentary on Orkney and its people. His interests and tastes were encyclopaedic, ranging from the fort and Martello Tower at Long Hope to social conditions and attitudes in the various islands. But from our point of view there is nothing to beat his description of the notorious Pentland Firth. The first encounter took place on 14 August, the day they were prevented by extreme tides from reaching the lighthouse:

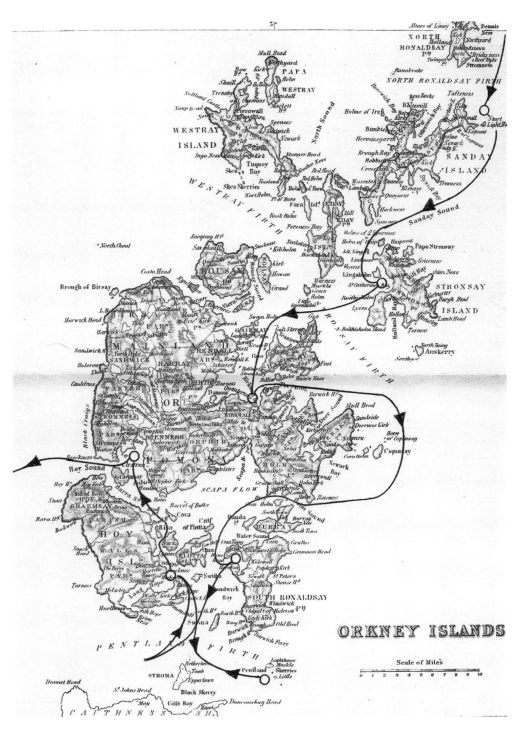

Approximate course of the Pharos among the Orkney Islands, 11 to 17 August 1814.

Enter the Pentland Firth, so celebrated for the strength and fury of its tides, which is boiling even in this pleasant weather; we see a large ship battling with this heavy current, and although with all her canvas set and a breeze, getting more and more involved … The breeze dies away between two wicked little islands called Swona and Stroma … Both islands have dangerous reefs and whirlpools, where, even, in this fine day, the tide rages furiously. Indeed, the large high unbroken billows, which at every swell hide from our deck each distant object, plainly intimate what a dreadful current this must be when vexed by high or adverse winds.

The next day they managed to get from Long Hope to the lighthouse and back, accompanied by a pilot-boat, and experienced at first hand some of the most treacherous tidal waters in the world:

Notwithstanding the fair weather, we have a specimen of the violence of the floodtide, which forms whirlpools on the shallow sunken rocks by the islands of Swoma and Stroma, and in the deep water makes strange, smooth, whirling, and swelling eddies, called by the sailors "wells". We run through the Wells of Tuftile in particular, which, in the least stress of weather, wheel a large ship round and round, without respect either to helm or sails … The bursting of waves in foam around these strange eddies has a bewildering and confused appearance, which it is impossible to describe. Get off the Skerries about ten o'clock, and land easily; it is the first time a boat has got there for several days.

Scott discovered that Muckle Skerry, the largest of the four skerries on which Thomas Smith had built his two lighthouse towers 20 years earlier, was a flattish 60-acre island surrounded by rocks, ravines, and blowholes, accessible only by steps cut into the rock.

Muckle Skerry and the two towers of Pentland Skerries Lighthouse (Paul A. Lynn).

Today's Stromness harbour makes a bright, well-ordered scene (Geograph/ Stuart Wilding).

About 50 cattle grazed the short grass and could only be got on and off with the greatest difficulty. There was no fresh water except what the rain left in pools. Scott noted that the lighthouse was 'too low' – it would be rebuilt and upgraded by Robert Stevenson some years later – and that its keeper was:

> an old man-of-war's-man, of whom Mr Stevenson observed that he was a great swearer when he first came; but after a year or two's residence in this solitary abode, became a changed man.

The lighthouse inspection completed, *Pharos* returned to Long Hope and continued to Stromness Bay where she anchored among whaling vessels. They were hemmed in, for the first time in Orkney, by impressive hills and cliffs. The next day was largely spent exploring local lochs, the famous Standing Stones of Stenness (which Scott considered second only to Stonehenge), and the island of Hoy. The small town of Stromness occupied their last day in Orkney and made an impression that was, to say the least, uninspiring:

> No letters from Abbotsford or Edinburgh. Stromness is a little dirty straggling town, which cannot be traversed by a cart, or even by a horse, for there are stairs up and down, even in the principal streets … We climb, by steep and dirty lanes, an eminence rising above the town, and commanding a fine view. An old hag lives in a wretched cabin on this height, and subsists by selling winds. Each captain of a merchantman, between jest and earnest, gives the old woman sixpence, and she boils her kettle to procure a favourable gale.

Captain Wilson coaxed *Pharos* out of Stromness Bay into Hoy Sound that evening, no doubt hoping that Bessy Millie would conjure up one of her favourite gales. And sure enough, by next morning they were well on their way to Cape Wrath, the northwest extremity of mainland Scotland. It had been an extraordinary 20 days since leaving Edinburgh, always challenging and sometimes dangerous, and his passengers would remember it for the rest of their lives.

It is hard to escape the thought that Walter Scott was the least prepared of all the passengers to face the realities of life in the Northern Isles. He may have been at ease with the VIPs of Lerwick and Kirkwall, but the poverty and lifestyles of many islanders was almost incomprehensible to a cultured member of the Edinburgh elite. Yet he managed to distil much of the experience for subsequent use, especially in his historical novel *The Pirate*, a romantic adventure set around Shetland's Sumburgh Head and its notorious Roost. The headland, from which he had sent a giant boulder crashing into the sea before sliding down a grassy slope on his bottom, had clearly captured his imagination. It would get its Stevenson lighthouse a year before his 1822 novel hit the bookshops of Edinburgh.

Robert Stevenson was far better prepared for the voyage and the sights it provided. He was used to making annual inspections around the Scottish coast and had learned a lot about conditions in Orkney while building the lighthouse at Start Point. He loved fierce gales and wild seas, scrambles among rocks and high cliffs, and the challenge of life aboard a lighthouse yacht. Now a man of 42 at the height of his powers, he was the professional with a job to do, whereas Scott must have seemed to his fellow passengers like a man on a pleasure trip. And while Scott had all the sensibilities of a poet, Stevenson was a man of action who spared himself, and those around him, no hardship in pursuit of his duties. He was undoubtedly aware of economic and social conditions in the Northern Isles, and may have cared about them; but his work was ultimately directed towards protecting the lives of mariners, and any compassion he felt was probably directed offshore.

Onshore, the first half of the 19th century became notorious for the Highland Clearances, one of the darkest chapters in Scottish history. Profitable sheep were substituted for unprofitable people over large areas of the Highlands and Islands. The 'First Wave' of clearances began in the 1780s, the decade in which the Northern Lighthouse Board was set up to light the coasts of Scotland, and was in full flow by 1814. It is tempting to speculate what effect, if any, it had on Scott and his companions aboard the *Pharos*.

Initially, the intention of most landowners was to shift impoverished tenants to the coastal fringes of their estates, encouraging them to catch fish and farm kelp (seaweed); but as time went by many were simply evicted and forced to emigrate. The most infamous programme of clearances occurred on the vast Sutherland Estates in the far north of Scotland between 1809 and 1821. Elizabeth, Countess of Sutherland, who was advantageously married to Lord Stafford, one of wealthiest men in Britain, decided on a comprehensive set of clearances that eventually replaced nearly 15 thousand people with sheep. The methods used to evict them, particularly those of her agent Patrick Sellar, were disgraceful; and by a strange coincidence 1814 became known as the "Year of the Burnings" in which people were scorched out of their homes. Among the worst afflicted were the inhabitants of Strathnaver, who were forced to a new coastal settlement about 30 miles east of Cape Wrath. The Countess had it named Bettyhill after herself.

The *Pharos* left Orkney on 17 August 1814 and must have passed within sight of Bettyhill the next morning. Smoke was probably rising tragically from the hinterland, but captain and crew were focused on reaching Cape Wrath where Robert Stevenson was to conduct a survey. Unfortunately Bessy Millie's charm began to fail as the wind strengthened and veered westerly; two of the Commissioners decided to stay in their berths but a third sat with Scott upon the deck 'like great bears, wrapt in watch-cloaks, the sea flying over us every now and then'. *Pharos* ran for shelter at Loch Eriboll, 15 miles beyond Bettyhill, and stayed there for two days. Cape Wrath had to await a more favourable wind.

Scott does not mention the Countess of Sutherland or Bettyhill, preferring to deflect concern towards Lord Reay and his somewhat smaller estates around Cape Wrath. Sheep were again in prospect, and to maximise the land's rental income it would be necessary for his lordship:

> to turn out several hundred families who have lived under him and his
> fathers for many generations, and the swords of whose fathers probably
> won the lands from which he is now expelling them .... Wealth is no
> doubt Strength in a country, while all is quiet and governed by law, but
> on any altercation or internal commotion, it ceases to be strength, and
> is only the means of tempting the strong to plunder the possessors.
> Much may be said on both sides.

Scott is clearly conflicted. Perhaps it is what we should expect from a distinguished poet who was also a member of Scotland's Tory establishment, a man who a few years later would accept a baronetcy and take a leading part in welcoming King George IV to Edinburgh, there to dress the monarch ridiculously in tartan in an attempt to revitalise the Union. His political stance was broadly that of the paternalistic one-nation Toryism later espoused by Benjamin Disraeli: all members of society, including the wealthy, should receive mutual benefits in return for mutual obligations. But Scott's worried comments certainly look like writing on the wall for the tenants of Lord Reay; and sure enough, 15 years later his lordship's estates passed into the hands of 'the noble family of Sutherland'.

The first wave of clearances was over by the 1820s. It was followed by a period of consolidation as landowners waited nervously for the crofting population to settle into fishing and kelping. However the national economy was in a parlous state after the Napoleonic wars, the kelp industry collapsed, small tenants were increasingly poverty-stricken and, to add insult to other injuries, the dreaded potato blight struck in 1836. Although efforts by benevolent landlords, charities, and the government prevented widespread starvation, the less scrupulous used the crisis as a further opportunity to organise their estates along more profitable lines. A second wave of clearances began, and continued on and off for decades. Some landowners simply evicted unwanted tenants, and chartered ships to transport them to distant lands.

The intrepid passengers aboard the *Pharos* approached the remaining four weeks of their voyage in the same spirit of uncomplaining adventure they had shown in Shetland, Fair Isle, and Orkney. There were several more sites for Robert Stevenson to survey including the awesome headland at Cape Wrath, and existing lighthouses for

The headland at Cape Wrath, surveyed by Robert Stevenson during the voyage of the Pharos in 1814. He completed the lighthouse in 1828 (Geograph/Colin Wheatley).

him to inspect as the vessel skirted the western coasts and threaded her way among the Hebridean islands.

One of the bravest decisions made by Captain Wilson was to anchor off Skerryvore, the notorious reef 12 miles from the coast of Tiree that was crying out for a lighthouse, and land a party on the rock in stormy conditions. The night before, the wind had been 'exceedingly tyrannical', the dishes and glasses in the steward's cupboards had become 'locomotive', and it was almost impossible for passengers to stay in their bunks, let alone stand upright. As dawn broke Scott found the *Pharos* beating to windward off the Isle of Tiree while Robert Stevenson argued with colleagues about the wisdom of attempting a landing. It was eventually agreed to accept his judgement, whatever it might be, rather than prolong the agony. Scott and two Commissioners risked their lives by jumping into a small boat with the determined engineer and headed for the rocks:

> Pull through a very heavy swell with great difficulty, and approach a tremendous surf dashing over black pointed rocks. Our rowers, however, get the boat into a quiet creek between two rocks, where we contrive to land well wetted. I saw nothing remarkable in my way, excepting several seals, which we might have shot, but, in the doubtful circumstances of the landing, we did not care to bring guns. We took possession of the rock in name of the Commissioners, and generously

A Victorian engraving of Alan Stevenson's majestic Skerryvore, completed in 1844 (Wikipedia).

bestowed our own great names on its crags and creeks. The rock was carefully measured by Mr S. It will be a most desolate position for a lighthouse – the Bell Rock and Eddystone a joke to it, for the nearest land is the wild island of Tyree, at fourteen miles' distance. So much for the Skerry Vhor.

It says a lot about Robert Stevenson's character that he championed the building of a lighthouse on Skerryvore and, in stark contrast to his poet companion, considered it a lesser challenge than the Bell Rock. But 30 years would pass before the tower was built, and then only thanks to stupendous efforts by Alan, his eldest son.

As the voyage of the *Pharos* draws to a close, we are left in awe of the difficulties and dangers posed by the Northern Lighthouse Board's inspection of the Scottish lights. Yet the annual commitment was carried out by Robert Stevenson with unfailing zest and enthusiasm throughout his tenure. He simply loved the physical challenge. However it was to prove far less attractive to his sons, and especially Alan whose health was really not up to the demands. As the years went by the number of lighthouses increased steadily, and more were built on small islands in Orkney and Shetland including Auskerry, Copinsay, Out Skerries and Muckle Flugga. The inspections continued to involve perilous landings among rocks in small rowing boats. Onshore tracks were poor, roads non-existent. The only major improvement between 1814 and 1858, when David and Thomas Stevenson completed Muckle Flugga, was the widespread introduction of steam propulsion for ocean-going vessels, which greatly reduced delays and changes of schedule caused by vagaries of the wind.

The voyage of the *Pharos* ended at Greenock on the Clyde on 8 September 1814, and her passengers transferred to a new-fangled river steamboat for Glasgow:

We took leave of our little yacht under the repeated cheers of the sailors, who had been much pleased with their erratic mode of travelling about, so different from the tedium of a regular voyage.

> After we reached Glasgow – a journey which we performed at the
> rate of about eight miles an hour, and with a smoothness of motion
> which probably resembles flying – we supped together and prepared
> to separate.

Walter Scott ends with a touching tribute to his fellow passengers who, in spite of very different interests and a severe lack of personal space aboard the lighthouse yacht, had got on famously. He had enjoyed as much pleasure as in any six weeks of his life with 'a succession of wild and uncommon scenery, good-humour on board, and objects of animation and interest when we went ashore'. Edinburgh may have seemed a little dull on his return, apart from its predictable city buzz and the continuing literary hullaballoo surrounding the publication of *Waverley*. Presumably Robert Stevenson went straight back to work in the office.

5 Eye witness: Robert Louis Stevenson

Our second eye witness, one of the world's favourite storytellers, has a special claim to attention. Not only was he a grandson of Robert Stevenson and son of Thomas Stevenson, but he endured several years of engineering apprenticeship totally unsuited to his talents and inclinations. In later life he looked back at his family members with a mixture of fascination, regret, and admiration; and, fortunately for us, he wrote about them.

We now move forward from 1814, the year of Walter Scott's voyage aboard the *Pharos*, to the second half of the 19th century, almost exactly the lifespan of Robert Louis Stevenson (1850–94). This engineer manqué, rebel author of classics including *Treasure Island*, *Kidnapped*, and *The Strange Case of Dr Jekyll and Mr Hyde*, has left us some fascinating memories of his engineering relatives and the experiences to which they subjected him. Like Scott he gained an international reputation as a writer, but the two men could hardly be more different as characters: one, a member of Edinburgh's Tory establishment, an extrovert who was equally at ease with the islanders of Orkney and Shetland and the Scottish elite; the other, a somewhat tortured individual who travelled extensively, seeking health as well as exotic cultures, and ended up in the South Pacific.

The young RLS with his father Thomas; and the family home in Heriot Row, Edinburgh (Wikipedia).

RLS, as he is often known, was born to Maggie and Thomas Stevenson at 8 Howard Place, Edinburgh, in November 1850. As already noted, the much-loved child suffered greatly from delicate health which forced the family into two house moves by the time he was six – firstly to 1 Inverleith Terrace, which proved unacceptably damp and chilly, then to sunnier 17 Heriot Row. His own childhood memories, recalled many years later, make painful reading:

> All this time, be it borne in mind, my health was of the most precarious description. Many winters I never crossed the threshold; but used to lie on my face on the nursery floor, chalking or painting in water-colours the pictures in the illustrated newspapers; or sit up in bed, with a little shawl pinned about my shoulders, to play with bricks, or dolls, or what not … My ill-health principally chronicles itself by the terrible long nights that I lay awake, troubled continually with a hacking, exhausting cough, and praying for sleep or morning from the bottom of my shaken little body.

His father would come up to his bedroom and sit by the bedside, consoling him after nightmares and trying to distract him with stories of coachmen and innkeepers. But Thomas Stevenson was increasingly busy with lighthouse engineering and Maggie had health problems of her own, so the person who did most to soothe the child's nerves during this period was his nurse Alison Cunningham, 30-year-old daughter of a weaver, who took the strain off his parents by joining the household in 1852. She was to stay with them for 20 years.

The loving care 'Cummy' gave RLS in sickness earned his eternal gratitude. Later he would versify her as 'my second mother, my first wife, the angel of my infant life'. Unfortunately she also had a darker side, an even stricter interpretation of Scottish Protestantism than his parents, and was quite capable of producing Calvinist stories of damnation when he was well. He developed an extreme terror of Hell and lay awake at night 'weeping for Jesus', terrified of falling asleep and plunging into the abyss. Later he worried about the spiritual welfare of parents who played cards and gave dinner parties, activities condemned in the religious biographies on which he had been fed.

In fact Thomas Stevenson, in spite of bouts of spiritual melancholy and the occasional religious outburst, had a considerable sense of fun. A wide range of hobbies and interests, artistic and scientific, counteracted any tendency towards fanaticism. Maggie, tall, elegant and fond of amusement, was by nature an optimist, and even Cummy could at times be 'full of life and merriment', her austere readings from the Bible and *The Pilgrim's Progress* set against the adventure stories of R.M. Ballantyne and the pleasures of *Robinson Crusoe*. It is easy to imagine RLS growing up confused by the mixed messages received from such a complicated household.

We may also wonder how such a sensitive and sickly child could possibly have been pointed in the direction of lighthouse engineering by his family as he approached maturity. After all, his father had favoured bookish pursuits when young – pursuits which had exasperated his own father Robert – and had entered the family business more or less by default. His scholarly uncle Alan, another sensitive and artistic Stevenson, had only agreed to become an engineer after a prolonged battle with the indomitable Robert, and was forced by chronic ill-health to relinquish his appointment as Engineer to the Northern Lighthouse Board in 1853 at the age of 46. Surely the family's recent experience should have warned it against propelling the painfully vulnerable boy towards professional engineering, with all the mental and physical resilience it demanded? The answer inevitably lies in the formidable character of Robert, founder of the dynasty, a man who remembered poverty in his own childhood, had achieved international celebrity for his Bell Rock masterpiece, and assumed that his male descendants could do nothing better than follow in his footsteps. Robert died in 1850, it was also the year in which RLS was born. The patriarch was to cast a lengthy shadow.

Continuing health problems meant that RLS had a fragmented education, with a succession of schools and private tutors. Consistency was further jeopardised by his father, whose lifelong contempt for traditional education did nothing to encourage academic success. Rummaging around in secondhand bookshops was time well spent, formal study quite another. At one point Thomas even declared that the only thing a boy needed to do at school was 'sit on his bum'.

Perhaps unsurprisingly, RLS was a late reader; but he became increasingly convinced that if any profession was to engage him it would be that of a wordsmith:

> All through my boyhood and youth, I was known and pointed out for
> the pattern of an idler; and yet I was always busy on my own private
> end, which was to learn to write. I kept always two books in my pocket,
> one to read, one to write in.

He also developed a love of imaginative games, solitary when ill, shared with cousins when well – even though he was invariably 'exhausted to death by the evening'. Foremost among playmates was 'Cousin Bob', Robert Mowbray Stevenson, the only son of Alan and Margaret Stevenson and three years his senior. As early as 1856 Bob was invited to stay and share the delights of a toy theatre; later he studied art and had a major effect on Robert Louis' imaginative development, encouraging him to break away from the social conventions and religious observances of life at 17 Heriot Row.

The young RLS often spent holidays with his maternal grandparents in Colinton, then a village outside Edinburgh, where his grandfather, the Reverend Lewis Balfour, was minister of the local parish church. He mixed with a veritable bevy of cousins on the Balfour side, some of them returning from India where their parents were working. The tribe was cared for and entertained by the reverend's unmarried daughter Jane, and RLS found the light-hearted atmosphere in the Manse a godsend:

> Out of my reminiscences of life in that dear place, all the morbid
> and painful elements have disappeared. I remember no more nights
> of storm; no more terror or sickness … That was my golden age …

There is something so fresh and wholesome about all that went on at Colinton, compared with what I recollect of the town that I can hardly, even in my own mind, knit the two chains of reminiscences together.

If the tense atmosphere back home in Heriot Row tended towards hypochondria, it was at least partly due to Maggie Stevenson who suffered from a 'weak chest' and was often advised to rest. Fortunately Thomas, ever attentive to the needs of his adored wife and son, took to renting furnished houses in Scotland's health resorts in the summer months; later, he would escort them to France to recuperate from the rigours of the Scottish winter, juggling the needs of family with his professional responsibilities.

At the age of 13 RLS spent a year at a boarding school in Isleworth near London, followed by Robert Thomson's school in Edinburgh. He enrolled in the Arts faculty at Edinburgh University in the autumn of 1867 and was pressured to study civil engineering. But it was simply not to be. He proved hopeless at concentrating on anything technical, and began to rebel against the assumption that he would automatically enter the family profession. The seeds of revolt had already been sown by Cousin Bob, and early experiences of engineering, academic and practical, did nothing to bring him back into line.

The simmering academic issue came to a head when he started to take Professor Fleeming Jenkin's third-year engineering classes at the university. He had already shown minimal enthusiasm for mathematics and natural philosophy, but engineering science was so foreign to his instincts that he stopped attending. The truancy was noted by his professor, who initially refused to issue an attendance certificate, declaring that 'It is quite useless for you to come to me, Mr Stevenson. There may be doubtful cases, there is no doubt about yours. You have simply not attended my class'. RLS pleaded fervently and a form of words was eventually found to satisfy his father. Years later he wrote of the shame attaching to the deception, which formed the 'bitter beginning' of an unlikely but lasting friendship with the tolerant academic.

His practical experiences started at two harbours on the east coast of Scotland – Anstruther, a small coastal town about 50 miles from Edinburgh, and Wick in the far north. As part of an apprenticeship with his father the 17-year-old was expected to familiarise himself with the family's harbour projects, and the university vacation of 1868 found him in Anstruther. In an essay written many years later, he noted:

> my father at the time was visiting the harbour lights of Scotland; and it was decided he should take me along with him around a portion of the shores of Fife; my first professional tour, my first journey in the complete character of man, without the help of petticoats.

But the coast of Fife left him cold:

> It has no beauty to recommend it, being a low, sea-salted, wind-vexed promontory; trees very rare ... Here it was that my first tour of inspection

A delightful scene in modern Anstruther. The historic Reaper, *a so-called Fifie, lies outside the Scottish Fisheries Museum. She was used as a fishing boat in Shetland for many years (Geograph/James Allan).*

> began, early on a bleak easterly morning. There was a crashing run of sea upon the shore, I recollect, and my father and the man of the harbour light must sometimes raise their voices to be audible.

Actually it was worse than that because he began, for the first time, to realise that the work of a civil engineer included:

> hanging about with the east wind humming in my teeth, and my hands (I make no doubt) in my pockets. I looked for the first time upon that tragi-comedy of the visiting engineer which I have seen so often re-enacted on a more important stage.

His doubts and difficulties were relayed back to his parents in a series of letters which pulled no punches. To his mother he wrote:

> I am utterly sick of this grey, grim, sea-beaten hole. I have a little cold in my head which makes my eyes sore; and you can't tell how utterly

sick I am and how anxious to get back among trees and flowers and something less meaningless than this bleak fertility.

He was rather more careful with his father, who naturally hoped that the young apprentice would find the work experience to his taste. But even here RLS was at times remarkably frank, showing that his close and open relationship with Thomas remained, for the time being, intact. It says a lot for his worried parents that they accepted his unenthusiastic letters and tried to look on the bright side.

In a later essay, 'Random Memories – the Education of an Engineer', he described the next port of call, the 'sub-arctic' town of Wick, where (as we have already seen) his father and his uncle David were constructing a huge breakwater to provide shelter for fishing vessels. Unfortunately the countryside around Wick enchanted him even less than the coast of Fife:

> You can never have dwelt in a country more unsightly than that part of Caithness, the land faintly swelling, faintly falling, not a tree, not a hedgerow, the fields divided by single slate stones set upon their edge, the wind always singing in your ears and (down the long road that led nowhere) thrumming in the telegraph wires. Only as you approached the coast was there anything to stir the heart. The plateau broke down to the North Sea in formidable cliffs, the tall out-stacks rose like pillars ringed about with surf, the coves were over-brimmed with clamorous froth, the sea-birds screamed, the wind sang in the thyme on the cliff's edge …. As for Wick itself, it is one of the meanest of man's towns, and situate certainly on the baldest of God's bays. It lives for herring …

Wick's great fleet of herring boats, crewed by Gaelic speakers from the Outer Hebrides, dominated the small town. In a bad year when catches were meagre it could become a dangerous place with fights and riots. On his arrival RLS noticed a gunboat in the bay, standing ominously by.

Work on the massive breakwater had started in 1863 and already extended 1,000 feet out into Wick Bay, ending in water 30 feet deep. Divers were busy toiling unseen on the

Harbour works at Wick have a long history of storm damage. This postcard is from 1913 (Wikipedia).

foundations, clad in cumbersome diving suits and helmets, kept alive from above with air supplied by hand-cranked pumps, and RLS was fascinated:

> To go down in the diving-dress, that was my absorbing fancy; and with the countenance of a certain handsome scamp of a diver, Bob Bain by name, I gratified the whim. It was gray, harsh, easterly weather, the swell ran pretty high, and out in the open there were "skipper's daughters," when I found myself at last on the diver's platform, twenty pounds of lead upon each foot and my whole person swollen with ply and ply of woollen underclothing. One moment, the salt wind was whistling round my night-capped head; the next, I was crushed almost double under the weight of the helmet. As that intolerable burthen was laid upon me, I could have found it in my heart (only for shame's sake) to cry off from the whole enterprise. But it was too late. The attendants began to turn the hurdy-gurdy, and the air to whistle through the tube; some one screwed in the barred window of the vizor; and I was cut off in a moment from my fellow-men; standing there in their midst, but quite divorced from intercourse: a creature deaf and dumb, pathetically looking forth upon them from a climate of his own.

The chief lesson of his submarine adventure was that the intolerable weight of the diving suit disappeared once under water. Large blocks of stone could be handled with relative ease. He began to move around, accompanied by Bob Bain, and finally gave a little push-up with his toes:

> Up I soared like a bird, my companion soaring at my side ... Of a sudden, my ascending head passed into the trough of a swell. Out of the green, I shot at once into a glory of rosy, almost of sanguine light — the multitudinous seas incarnadined, the heaven above a vault of crimson. And then the glory faded into the hard, ugly daylight of a Caithness autumn, with a low sky, a gray sea, and a whistling wind. Bob Bain had five shillings for his trouble, and I had done what I desired. It was one of the best things I got from my education as an engineer.

Actually it was one of the very few things he got – and it had nothing to do with lighthouses. The teenage tyro found the rest of the work on the site exhausting and uncongenial, and any design calculations requested by his father impossible. At one point he wrote asking 'what is the weight of a square foot [sic] of salt water? And how many pounds are there to a ton?' – queries that could hardly have increased Thomas's confidence in formal education.

A year after Anstruther and Wick, with another unproductive university session behind him, RLS followed family tradition by accompanying his father on a fortnight's inspection tour of Orkney and Shetland lighthouses. By 1869 there were 11 major lights,

Wick harbour today: still battered by waves, but in fine shape (Geograph/ Dorcas Sinclair).

from Pentland Skerries in the south to Muckle Flugga in the far north, and the voyage covered six of them – the combined fruits of the labours of his grandfather Robert, uncles Alan and David, and father Thomas. Needless to say, he was nowhere near as enthusiastic about the Northern Isles and its lighthouses as Walter Scott had been half a century earlier and he left us with nothing to rival Scott's delightful 1814 travelogue. However he did manage two lengthy letters to his concerned mother, prefaced by a caveat that they would cover his 'sore journeying and perilous peregrination'.

The first letter, dated 18 June 1869, was written aboard the lighthouse steamer as she reached the southern Orkney islands. They had crossed the notorious Pentland Firth and were lucky because although the vessel 'rolled a little, the swell was nothing'. Next morning they inspected the Cantick Head Lighthouse, built by David and Thomas Stevenson on the island of Hoy in 1858, and found 'the faces of the men sufficient for inspection. You could see they were at their ease. The flag was hoist while we were in'. But he gives no details, either because he took little notice or because he thought they would bore his mother. We may take this as a shot across the bows: from now on the apprentice engineer ignores the inspection aspects of the tour, concentrating instead on the sights and experiences that appealed to his literary imagination and, hopefully, Maggie's interests.

By noon they had visited the Hoy High and Hoy Low Lighthouses ('in good order, the view was very pretty') built by Alan Stevenson in 1851; and by mid-afternoon were safely anchored in Scapa Flow, from where they landed and set off cross-country to Kirkwall. Like Walter Scott, RLS discovered that 'the glory of Kirkwall, as of Salisbury, lies about its Cathedral'. He gives it the best part of 1,500 words – not bad for a letter to a mother, even one written by a wordsmith – and sums up with a flourish:

> I know nothing so suggestive of legend, so full of superstition, so stimulating to a weird imagination, as the nooks and corners and bye-ways of such a church as St Magnus in Kirkwall.

Pharos V, *in service with the Northern Lighthouse Board between 1854 and 1874.*

But his next experience was altogether less delightful:

> We then went down to the pier, where indeed we had a lamentable wakening and grievous revocation from Middle-Ages dreamland to everyday vulgarity and affectation. A London engineer has erected an iron jetty, like the ornamental bridge over the water in a cockney tea-garden – a gimcrack lane of carven lamp-posts – infinitely neat and infinitely shaky – a nursemaids' walk, that might have done at Greenwich, projecting into the easterly surge from Pomona the mainland of Orkney. Alas! alas!

By evening they were 'running to Shetland', with Fair Isle visible ahead and the lighthouse tower of North Ronaldsay 'standing up clear behind with no land for it to stand upon'. It was approaching midnight, the steamer was rolling and pitching gently, they were within a few days of the summer solstice, and RLS was able 'to read small type on the bridge with the utmost ease'.

The next section of his letter was written the following morning at Bluemull Sound, the strait of water that divides Yell from Unst, Shetland's most northerly island. On the way they had visited the Out Skerries Lighthouse, built by David and Thomas in 1858 as a replacement for the temporary light of 1854 – but, once again, nothing about the inspection itself, only that 'the keepers took us down to show us rock torn up by the sea'.

Three Orkney lighthouses visited by RLS and inspected by his father in 1869: left, Cantick Head (Geograph/Oliver Dixon); Hoy High (centre) and Hoy Low (right) (Geograph/Mike Pennington).

Far more interesting were the antics of 'sea birds called in local jargon Spotted Allans, who never fish for themselves, but pursue the gulls who catch anything and make them give it up' – no doubt the skuas, or bonxies, so well-known to today's visitors to northern Shetland.

And now comes the most interesting part of the letter for the pharologist – a visit to Muckle Flugga and its lighthouse, built by his father and his uncle David 11 years before, and originally known as North Unst. Once again, RLS ignores the inspection, merely commenting that the lighthouse 'was in good order'; but its dramatic and hazardous situation, the recent history surrounding it, and the realisation that little but Arctic ice lay to the north, finally fired his imagination:

> The coast beyond the embouchure of Blumel Sound, the western seaboard of Unst, is wild and rugged, dark cliffs riven with inky voes and caverns, white with sea birds, marked here and there by natural arches, and crowned with round hills of sere sun-burnt grass. In about half an hour we sighted North Unst Lighthouse, the most northern dwelling house in Her Majesty's dominium. The mainland rises higher, with great seams and landslips; and from the norwestern corner runs out a string of shelving ledges, with a string of green and purple seaweed and a boil of white foam about their feet. The lighthouse stands on the highest – 190 feet above the sea; and there is only an uninhabited reef called the Out Stack between it and the Faroe Islands … We steamed round between the lighthouse and the Out Stack … with a great long swell from the northward splashing about her bows …
>
> We were pulled into the creek … between the Lighthouse and the other rock, down the centre of which runs a line of reef … This is very narrow, little broader than a knife edge; but its ridge has been

cut into stone steps and laid with iron grating and railed with an iron railing. It was here that we landed, making a leap between the swells at a rusted iron ladder laid slant-wise against the raking side of the ridge. Before us a flight of stone steps led up the two hundred feet to the lighthouse in its high yard-walls across whose foot the sea had cast a boulder weighing twenty tons. On one side is a slippery face of clear sound rock; and on the other a chaos of pendulous boulder and rotten stone. On either side there was no vegetation save tufts of sea-pink in the crevices and a little white lichen on the lee faces. The lighthouse was in good order. We are now returning by Blumel Sound to Sunday at Lerwick.

It is by far his most informative and positive passage so far, at least as far as lighthouses are concerned.

Lerwick produced an eclectic mix of impressions, as it had in Walter Scott half a century earlier – narrow lanes climbing the hillside 'on long flights of ruinous steps'; Fort Charlotte, founded by Cromwell, overhanging the water at the north of the town and containing a jail and court-house where, a few days before, a young man had hanged himself rather than face a prison sentence for shooting ducks on Unst; smugglers of tobacco and brandy, insistent that their activities were a natural right; a midnight moon 'mirrored to perfection in the waters of the Sound'. The letter was signed, sealed, and sent off in haste to catch Lerwick's hesitant postal service. He immediately began a second one to his dear Mamma, describing more of Lerwick's curiosities.

The next morning, 21 June, they sailed from Lerwick and dropped anchor off Sumburgh Head for an inspection of the lighthouse built by his grandfather in 1821 ('We then visited the light and went on board again'). He was impressed by the nearby remains of the Jarlshof settlement, 'so often mentioned in *The Pirate*' – Walter Scott's novel written after his 1814 voyage. But the visit was quickly over and by late afternoon the steamer had called in at Fair Isle and was heading south for Orkney.

What did RLS make of Fair Isle, and what would he tell his mother? Half a century earlier Scott had formed strong impressions of the inhabitants: admiration for the men's skills at sailing and fishing and the women's at knitting; pleasure at their 'sober, good-humoured, and friendly' demeanour; and a general appreciation of their social cohesion and ability to keep the island's fragile economy above water. His only big problem was acceptance of the squalid conditions in which some of them lived. But perhaps these had improved by the summer of 1869?

It seems not, at least if Robert Louis' second letter to his mother is to be believed. Before describing the island's human condition he sets the geographical scene:

The coast of the Fair Isle is the wildest and most unpitying that we have yet seen. Continuous cliffs from one to four hundred feet high, torn by huge voes and echoing caverns, line the bare downs with scarcely a cove of sand or a practicable cleft in the belt of iron precipice. At intervals

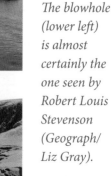

Dramatic cliff scenery of Fair Isle. The blowhole (lower left) is almost certainly the one seen by Robert Louis Stevenson (Geograph/ Liz Gray).

it runs out into strange peninsulas, square bluff headlands, and plumb faces of stone, tinged with the faint green of some sort of lichen.

Close by one of these was the long, bleak inlet into which the Duke of Medina Sidonia's vessel, the flagship of the great Armada, was driven in the storm. It was strange to think of the great old ship, with its gilded castle of a stern, its scroll-work and emblazoning and with a Duke of Spain on board, beating her brains out on the iron bound coast of the Fair Isle.

The only nobleman RLS met on Fair Isle was not a Spaniard there by accident, but a Briton there by design. Lord Teynham ambled down to the beach to meet the visitors off the *Pharos,* declaring himself 'a servant of the Lord Jesus Christ, come here to preach his word'. An elderly, ill-clothed, dishevelled gentleman, the date of his last shave needed 'a more daring conjecture than I am prepared to offer or at least to chronicle in black and white'. He had arrived a few days before in a sloop owned by Mr Bruce of Sumburgh in Shetland, who also owned Fair Isle, and was staying in the minister's house.

The visitors were escorted to a dilapidated schoolhouse, half-roofed with wreck-timber, and then to a more convincing visitor attraction – a blowhole in the cliff some 70 feet deep, with a great arched doorway onto the ocean – 'the noise of a stone dropped in reverberates with a hollow boom'. On the way back they entered a house divided in three: a byre, a kitchen, and 'the room'. None of the doors was above four feet high. Smoke from a fire eventually found its way through holes in the thatch, but meanwhile hung in blue clouds among the rafters. Basic furniture included Fair Isle armchairs with a wooden frame and a back of plaited straw. Rent was about £4 a year; for the whole island, exclusive of fishing, about £150.

Nearby they encountered three women, two young, one old and haggard, and a child, and asked if they could buy coloured stockings. But no – instead, the women argued about the age and sensibility of the child. Next stop the church, 'seated for two hundred and fifty', and a churchyard containing the remains of two of the oldest men ever to die on the island, aged 61 and 64. RLS opines that 'intermarriage and bad houses make them a weak lot; and almost none of the women, as I hear, have good eyes'. Finally to the store, which offered 'tea, teapots, linen and blankets, and quaint-patterned, parti-coloured knitted socks, cowls, gloves and mittens'. While they had been on tour another passenger from the *Pharos* visited the sick of the island and declared that of all the miserable people he had ever seen, they were the worst. Their only hope was in death.

RLS ends with a summary that must surely have shocked his mother:

> Beyond reach of all communication, receiving such stray letters as may come not once in six long months, with diseased bodies, and wretched homes, they drag out their lives in the wildest and most barren island of the north. Their crops, raised after hard labour from a cold and stony soil, can only support them for three months out of the twelve. Indeed their only life is from the sea. It is the sea that brings the fish to their nets: it is the sea that strews their shore with the spoils of wrecked vessels (thus we saw in the minister's house, a huge German musical box saved from the wreck of the Lessing).
>
> Leaving a great parcel of papers, we went on board again.

By next day, June 22, the *Pharos* was lying in Scrabster Roads off the north coast of mainland Scotland and it was time to sign off:

> This letter goes tonight: hoping all are well, Believe me, Ever your affectionate son, R.L. Stevenson.

What should we make of such a dismal account, far more negative than Walter Scott's half a century earlier? If beauty is in the eye of the beholder then so, presumably, is ugliness. To what extent is Robert Louis' view of Fair Isle tainted by his feelings toward the whole experience of travelling aboard the *Pharos* with his father, visiting a series of lighthouses that interested him little and threatened an unattractive career? Throughout the two letters to his mother, a remarkable total of 8,000 words, he mentions his father only once, in a single sentence about a church service they had attended in Lerwick – nothing whatsoever about Thomas's lighthouse inspections, health, conversation, or social interactions. Had father and son finally fallen out towards the end of a fortnight's 'sore journeying and perilous peregrination'? Perhaps the young apprentice had spent too much time 'hanging about with the east wind humming in my teeth, and my hands (I make no doubt) in my pockets', as in Anstruther the year before.

Fortunately we can check his account against some objective evidence on the Fair Isle of 1869. As previously noted, the Highland Clearances were already under way in 1814 when Walter Scott accompanied Robert Stevenson on his annual inspection of the Scottish lights; but Orkney, Fair Isle, and Shetland were not greatly affected, and when the *Pharos* continued along Scotland's northern coastline towards Cape Wrath and the Hebrides her passengers would not have seen much to upset them. True, Scott was aware of trouble on the Countess of Sutherland's estates, and rumours about Lord Reay's intentions, but his political stance and robust personality prevented an excess of soul-searching. It was the second wave of Clearances, which began in the 1840s and continued for decades, that became the real decimator of human populations, on small Scottish islands as well as huge mainland estates.

From historical records we know that Fair Isle's population, almost wiped out by smallpox in 1701, had recovered to about 200 by 1790. It then increased steadily, peaking at 380 in 1861 and stretching the island's resources to the limit. Indeed beyond the limit, because the following year 134 people were either forced, or chose, to swap Fair Isle for Nova Scotia.

So when RLS landed on Fair Isle in the summer of 1869 the island was still reeling from the recent clearance of a third of its people – and not just any third, but almost certainly those of able body, sound mind, and a gritty determination to start again in a new land 2,700 miles across the North Atlantic. Left behind would have been the elderly and the sick, including those 'whose only hope was death', and many broken families among an island population that had intermarried for generations. Not that all the remaining inhabitants were hopeless; some must have survived in body and spirit because they managed to rescue 465 passengers and one huge musical box from the German vessel *Lessing*, driven onto the rocks at Clavers Geo the year before as she headed from Bremerhaven towards New York. But they must have been traumatised by the recent past and fearful of the future.

Perhaps we may settle for a compromise and view RLS's letter to his mother as a tangled product of his own unhappiness and the actual state of Fair Isle, which had clearly deteriorated since Walter Scott's visit; and conclude that, although the island was hardly enjoying the fruits of Britain's industrial revolution, nor could it be flattered by a disconsolate youth returning to his home city for another dose of university lectures. Twenty three years would pass before two of his cousins, David A. and Charles Stevenson, enthusiastic professional engineers, helped lift Fair Isle's spirits with a fine pair of lighthouses.

The trials of Robert Louis Stevenson's apprenticeship were not yet over. In the next summer vacation he was dispatched to the small tidal island of Erraid just off the coast of Mull, from where he sailed to the fourth offshore Scottish rock to be crowned with a Stevenson lighthouse. Dubh Artach (formerly known as Dhu Heartach) sticks up like a sore thumb in the North Atlantic, 15 miles southwest of Mull. Waves almost 100 feet high have been recorded during Atlantic storms, generated by an extensive submarine valley that funnels them towards the rock. The dreaded Torran Rocks cover about 10 square miles in the same sea area, lurking menacingly below the surface 'like dragon's teeth'. The twin hazards destroyed an untold number of vessels plying between the port of Oban, America and the Baltic in the first half of the 19th century, and the need for a lighthouse became ever more pressing, especially in the winter of 1865–6 when storms wrecked 24 vessels in the seas between the islands of Mull, Colonsay and Islay.

Thomas Stevenson had first landed on Dubh Artach in June 1865 to conduct a survey. Work on the new lighthouse began in 1867, and by the time RLS arrived in 1870 construction was well under way. It must have taken considerable courage for the young apprentice to spend three weeks sailing back and forth between Erraid and the rock, even as a spectator, because by now he was tormented by doubts about a career in lighthouse engineering. In an essay written many years later he delighted in the isle of Erraid, but castigated the rock:

> An ugly reef is this of the Dhu Heartach; no pleasant assemblage of shelves, and pools, and creeks, about which a child might play for a whole summer without weariness, like the Bell Rock or the Skerryvore, but one oval nodule of black-trap, sparsely bedabbled with an inconspicuous focus, and alive in every crevice with a dingy insect between a slater and a bug. No other life was there but of sea-birds, and of the sea itself, that here ran like a mill-race, and growled about the outer reef for ever, and ever and again, in the calmest weather, roared and spouted on the rock itself.

Whether a child could 'play for a whole summer' on Bell Rock or Skerryvore seems highly questionable, and the comment would certainly have irritated his grandfather Robert and his uncle Alan had they lived to read it. In any case occasional literary flourishes could not hide the reality, and seven months after visiting Dubh Artach, with another miserable university session behind him, RLS finally took the future in his own hands. He announced his decision to abandon engineering in favour of authorship.

It came about in a dramatic way. In March 1871 he was encouraged – or more likely compelled – to read a paper 'On a New Form of Intermittent Light for Lighthouses' at a meeting of the Royal Scottish Society of Arts. The paper was well received, but a week later he marked the end of the University session by organising a supper for Professor Jenkin's engineering class, and spilled the beans. This was followed by a 'dreadful evening walk' with his father, who was distressed to hear that he had learned nothing:

> On being tightly cross-questioned … I owned I cared for nothing but literature. My father said that was no profession; but I might be called to the bar if I chose; so, at the age of 21, I began to study law.

The decision hardly came as a surprise to his family and, to his father's great credit, was not seriously questioned. No doubt Thomas recalled vividly his own youthful misgivings about engineering. His mother was probably relieved, noting in her diary that 'Lou thinks of being an advocate and not a civil engineer. Tom wonderfully resigned'. She must have been fully aware of her son's struggles, academic and practical, over the previous four years.

Dubh Artach Lighthouse as it stands today (photo: Ian Cowe).

The 21-year-old's long-suppressed inclinations now erupted in a dramatic change of lifestyle, aided and abetted by Cousin Bob who had just returned to Edinburgh after taking an Arts degree at Cambridge University. The two cousins, as fascinated by the artistic life as they were repelled by civil engineering, were keen to resume their friendship. RLS found Bob an ideal soulmate and confidant:

> The miserable isolation in which I had languished was no more in season, and I began to be happy ... I was done with the sullens for good; there was an end of greensickness for my life as soon as I had got a friend to laugh with.

Within two years RLS rejected his family's dour version of Christianity, questioned parental views on almost everything else, became a 'red-hot socialist', joined Bob as a member of a disreputable Edinburgh club, and presented himself to the world as a thoroughgoing bohemian. The emotional turmoil took a severe toll on his health and in 1873 he went to the south of France for a period of recuperation. But he was back in Edinburgh the following year to qualify as a lawyer, a profession he would never practise.

He and Bob continued to develop an intimate friendship, expressed in a remarkable series of letters covering mutual interests in art and literature. The two young men took to travelling in Europe, behaving controversially, and revelling in Bohemian artistic circles. Bob went on to become a dazzling conversationalist and respected art critic, although he never succeeded as an artist in his own right. In 1873 he had a tremendous row with

Thomas Stevenson, who accused him of undermining Robert Louis' Christian faith and destroying the family's happiness. This marked a low point in relationships; but RLS could never forget his childhood love for Thomas and Maggie – love that would blossom again when he became a successful author.

His engineering days over, RLS developed an ambiguous relationship with the family's profession. He had renounced socially valuable lighthouse engineering, a fresh-air world of sea, stone, iron, and glass, and substituted an unproven indoor talent needing only pen and paper. But he was fair-minded enough to admit that civil engineering had its attractions for someone with a love of the great outdoors:

> It takes a man into the open air; it keeps him hanging about harbour-sides, which is the richest form of idling; it carries him to wild islands; it gives him a taste of the genial dangers of the sea; it supplies him with dexterities to exercise; it makes demands upon his ingenuity; it will go far to cure him of any taste (if ever he had one) for the miserable life of cities.

The downside was that wild nature, ships, and sea must periodically be swapped for stool, desk and detailed calculation; it was a rare person who could strike and accept the necessary balance between 'genuine life' and office drudgery.

In the next few years RLS spent all his energies writing and travelling, often to continental Europe. In 1876 he met and fell in love with Fanny Osbourne, an American 11 years his senior who had taken her three children to Paris following her husband's infidelities and was studying art. She decided to return to America in 1878 and a year later he followed her, much against the advice of friends and family. Travelling almost penniless, as a steerage passenger to New York and overland in extreme discomfort to California, he arrived at death's door. Fanny nursed him back to something like health, and they married in 1880 even though he was still 'a mere complication of cough and bones'. Soon afterwards they returned to New York and sailed for Liverpool with her son Lloyd.

Fanny's charm, wit and independence helped patch up the strained relationship between her husband and his family. She was well aware of their bitter rows over religion and the distress caused by his decision to follow her to America, a journey Thomas had described as 'this sinful mad business'. Fortunately several months of family anguish ended when news of RLS's serious illness and impending marriage reached Edinburgh. It is greatly to his parents' credit that there were no further recriminations, probably because they realised that for the first time in many years their son was contented. Fanny made a quick conquest of her father-in-law and was treated as indulgently as a favourite daughter. Within a few months she was writing about Thomas and Maggie in moving terms:

> They are the best and noblest people in the world, both of them, and I can hardly write of them now without tears in my eyes. Every day, almost, I come upon fresh proofs of their thought for our comfort or pleasure.

  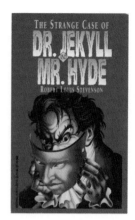

Fruits of the Bournemouth years: three of Robert Louis Stevenson's classic books (Wikipedia).

Over the next few years RLS and his wife searched Scotland and England for a home and environment suitable to his state of health, and took winter breaks in France. In 1884 they discovered a house in Bournemouth, celebrated in England for its balmy southern climate. RLS named it Skerryvore after his uncle Alan's graceful Hebridean lighthouse, an early sign that he wished to re-engage with his family background. It was to be their home for the three years in which he became a famous author.

His first major success, which brought critical acclaim at home and abroad, was *Treasure Island*. Originally serialised in a children's magazine, it was soon published as a book and became one of the most popular adventure stories of all time. Its success prompted *Kidnapped*, another buccaneering tale of sea, ships, and islands, also aimed at a young readership, which drew heavily on his experiences as an apprentice engineer on Mull and Dubh Artach. Written in Bournemouth and published in 1886, it has the main character David Balfour shipwrecked on the 'stoneyard' of the Torran Rocks and swimming ashore on the Isle of Erraid. Before the year was out the budding author signed a contract for *The Strange Case of*

RLS as an acknowledged storyteller; and his wife Fanny, photographed in about 1886 (Wikipedia).

*On Samoa: RLS with his wife and household, 1892; and the
RLS museum, a modern tourist attraction (Wikipedia).*

Dr Jekyll and Mr Hyde, a disturbing adult tale of the human psyche that avoided any mention of islands, lighthouses or stormy seas, and established his wider reputation.

These successes were achieved in spite of continuing ill health, and when his father died in 1887 RLS felt free to accept medical advice that he should try a complete change of climate. The family left Bournemouth and sailed for New York, where he spent a winter planning an adventurous cruise to the South Pacific the following year. In June 1888 they sailed from San Francisco in a chartered yacht, subsequently visiting Hawaii, the Gilbert Islands (now Kiribati), Tahiti, New Zealand, and the Samoan Islands. In 1890 RLS purchased a plot of about 400 acres in Samoa, where they decided to settle. Over the next few years he became involved in the local scene, social and political, and was able to continue writing and enjoying his reputation as a skilful teller of tales. He died suddenly from a cerebral haemorrhage in December 1894 at the age of 44, beloved by the locals who buried him on a mountaintop in a spot about as different from the city of his birth as is possible to imagine.

Robert Louis Stevenson's later years were spent so far from his family roots that we might suppose he forgot all about lighthouse engineering. But as middle age approached, perhaps sensing that his life was slipping prematurely away, he pondered his student rebellion and re-searched his family history. There was often a hint of regret, even guilt, in his reminiscences:

Say not of me that weakly I declined
The labours of my sires, and fled the sea,
The towers we founded and the lamps we lit,
To play at home with paper like a child.
But rather say: In the afternoon of time
A strenuous family dusted from its hands
The sand of granite, and beholding far
Along the sounding coast its pyramids
And tall memorials catch the dying sun,
Smiled well content, and to this childish task
Around the fire addressed its evening hours.

In an essay, 'Thomas Stevenson, Civil Engineer', penned soon after his father's death, RLS wrote movingly about the parent who had initially pushed him towards an engineering career but had always loved him. His recollections tell us a great deal about the character of the man who, with brother David, accepted the almost impossible challenges posed by Scottish lighthouse construction and, above all, Muckle Flugga.

Nearly 20 years after the dismal experiences of Anstruther, Wick, Orkney, Shetland, and Dhu Heartach, the newly-confident author, flushed with the success of *Treasure Island* and *Kidnapped,* was in forgiving mood. He recalls how Thomas was loved and admired in Edinburgh, but personally unknown elsewhere in spite of his international contributions to lighthouse engineering:

> wherever he went, in railway carriages or hotel smoking rooms, his strange, humorous, vein of talk, and his transparent honesty, raised him up friends and admirers. But to the general public and the world of London, except about the parliamentary committee rooms, he remained unknown. All the time, his lights were in every part of the world, guiding the mariner; his firm were consulting engineers to the Indian, the New Zealand, and the Japanese Lighthouse Boards, so that Edinburgh was a world centre for that branch of applied science; in Germany, he had been called "the Nestor of lighthouse illumination"; even in France, where his claims were long denied, he was at last, on the occasion of the late Exposition, recognised and medalled.

Thomas's service to mankind 'took on forms of which the public knows little and understands less'. His reputation, small at home, was huge abroad. A friend of RLS, on a visit to South America, was asked if he knew Mr Stevenson the author, whose works were much admired in Peru. The friend assumed the reference was to the storyteller, but not so: the Peruvian had never heard of *Treasure Island* or *Dr Jekyll and Mr Hyde* – what he had in mind were 'the volumes of the engineer'.

RLS acknowledges his father's work on Dhu Heartach and Skerryvore, 'the noblest of all extant deep-sea lights'; his collaboration with brother David in building many other Scottish lights and beacons; the harbour work at Wick, 'the chief disaster of my father's life'; and the improvement of rivers in England and Scotland. And then:

> It was about this nucleus of his professional labours that all my father's scientific inquiries and inventions centred; these proceeded from, and acted back upon, his daily business. Thus it was as a harbour engineer that he became interested in the propagation and reduction of waves … Storms were his sworn adversaries, and it was through the study of storms that he approached that of meteorology at large … But the great achievement of his life was, of course, in optics as applied to lighthouse illumination.

Thomas pioneered many improvements in revolving lights, although his claims aroused 'much painful controversy in France', homeland of the Fresnel brothers. Further inventions in lighthouse optics, especially his azimuthal condensing system, confirmed him one of mankind's benefactors and ensured that 'in all parts of the world a safer landfall awaits the mariner'. Such generous comments suggest that RLS was by now a man at peace, far too busy forging his own reputation to waste time blaming others for past insecurity and unhappiness.

We have already noted that as a child Thomas Stevenson loved writing stories and engaging in flights of fancy. The stark discipline of Victorian schools gave him a dislike for formal education and he was judged 'a reluctant pupil, wanting in arithmetic'. According to his son the weakness continued into adulthood:

> Thomas Stevenson was no mathematician. Natural shrewdness, a sentiment of optical laws, and a great intensity of consideration led him to just conclusions; but to calculate the necessary formulæ for the instruments he had conceived was often beyond him, and he must fall back on the help of others, notably on that of his cousin and lifelong intimate friend, emeritus Professor Swan, of St. Andrews, and his later friend, Professor P. G. Tait. It is a curious enough circumstance, and a great encouragement to others, that a man so ill equipped should have succeeded in one of the most abstract and arduous walks of applied science.

The intuitive engineer, a man who immersed himself in natural phenomena and developed a deeply-felt understanding for them, was still at heart a romantic.

The Stevenson engineers often held government appointments and regarded many of their inventions as public property, unprotected by patents. It was another reason for Thomas Stevenson's comparative obscurity outside his home city:

> for a patent not only brings in money, it infallibly spreads reputation; and my father's instruments enter anonymously into a hundred light-rooms, and are passed anonymously over in a hundred reports, where the least considerable patent would stand out and tell its author's story.

Finally, the engineer manqué considers his father's personal qualities:

> He was a man of a somewhat antique strain: with a blended sternness and softness that was wholly Scottish and at first somewhat bewildering; with a profound essential melancholy of disposition and (what often accompanies it) the most humorous geniality in company; shrewd and childish; passionately attached, passionately prejudiced; a man of many extremes, many faults of temper, and no very stable foothold for himself among life's troubles.

Yet he proved a wise adviser to friends and colleagues in trouble, a man of excellent taste who collected antique furniture and delighted in sunflowers, a traditional Tory softened by a chivalrous sentiment for women, and a devout member of the Church of Scotland, burdened by a morbid sense of life's fragility.

Although Thomas's innermost thoughts were always 'tinged with the Celtic melancholy', he revelled in the society of those he loved, the daily walks that took him far into the country with congenial friends, and 'dangling about the town from one old book-shop to another, scraping romantic acquaintance with every dog that passed'. His conversation, a mixture of common sense and freakish humour, was a perpetual delight to all that knew him 'before the clouds began to settle on his mind'. On the whole this complicated man had a happy life, and a fortunate death which 'at the last came to him unaware'.

Robert Louis Stevenson's intimate early relationship with his parents equipped him to write about Thomas with great insight and affection. But when it came to his grandfather, the founder of the family dynasty, he was on less familiar ground because the year of RLS's birth, 1850, coincided with Robert's death. Yet as the author grew older he became more and more interested in the grand old man's character and achievements, drawing on a remarkable collection of working notes and diaries, studiously maintained throughout the engineer's long career and backed up by a wealth of anecdotes passed down by family, friends, and colleagues in the lighthouse service. In *Records of a Family of Engineers*, and especially its chapter 'The service of the Northern Lights', RLS bequeathed us a goldmine of reminiscences about Robert's working life as well as some valuable snippets on Orkney and Shetland. It was written on Samoa and published posthumously in 1912, almost exactly a century after his grandfather had completed the Bell Rock Lighthouse.

He sets the scene with some comments about Robert's work as a young assistant to Thomas Smith, the Northern Lighthouse Board's first Engineer:

> It were hard to imagine a contrast more sharply defined than that between the lives of the men and women of this family: the one so chambered, so centred in the affections and the sensibilities; the other so active, healthy, and expeditious. From May to November, Thomas Smith and Robert Stevenson were on the mail, in the saddle, or at sea; and my grandfather, in particular, seems to have been possessed with a demon of activity in travel.

Constant travel by land and sea demanded a physical toughness that, in 19th-century Scotland, was almost superhuman. But in addition to his 'demon of activity', Robert was always on the lookout for new ideas, new experiences, new people to quiz:

> All his life long, his pen was in his hand, piling up a treasury of knowledge, preparing himself against all possible contingencies. Scarce anything fell under his notice but he perceived in it some

relation to his work, and chronicled it in the pages of his journal in his always lucid, but sometimes inexact and wordy, style. The Travelling Diary (so he called it) was kept in fascicles of ruled paper, which were at last bound up, rudely indexed, and put by for future reference.

The Travelling Diary contained a surprising medley of impressions, illustrating everything about civil engineering that RLS had found so uncongenial: its insistence on attention to technical detail; the recording of every observation for possible future use; a grasp of nature's forces and the properties of materials used to counteract them; and personal exposure to those forces in desolate places, often in great danger. At times his grandfather's literary limitations suggested 'a lusty old gentleman scrambling among tangle', yet the storyteller must have known he was tapping a source of engineering history that would be read long after his own demise.

Robert Stevenson considered it the duty of a professional engineer to design and construct his work to the highest possible standards. Fired by a remorseless personal ambition, a strong Protestant work ethic, and the certainty that the Northern Lighthouse Board's programme was carried out *in salutem omnium* ('for the safety of all'), he interpreted his duty with unflinching severity:

> in every detail and byway of his employments, he pursued the same ideal. Perfection (with a capital P and violently under-scored) was his design. A crack for a penknife, the waste of 'six-and-thirty shillings', 'the loss of a day or a tide', in each of these he saw and was revolted by the finger of the sloven; and to spirits intense as his, and immersed in vital undertakings, the slovenly is the dishonest, and wasted time is instantly translated into lives endangered.

RLS must surely have come to regard his famous grandfather as a workaholic. It was probably as well for both of them that they never met on a professional stage.

Robert may have been difficult to work with, but he inspired great loyalty in colleagues who appreciated that, like a great army commander, he expected every bit as much of himself as he ever did of them. On succeeding Thomas Smith as Engineer to the Northern Lighthouse Board in 1808, he conducted the annual lighthouse inspections with military precision. Sloppiness in others was simply not tolerated. It was a reign of tough love, based on the old-fashioned paternalistic ideal of a boss demanding high standards in return for fair treatment and, when necessary, personal advice and support in times of trouble.

An endearing characteristic of Robert Stevenson was his social acceptance of all sorts and conditions of men, providing they aspired to his standards of honesty and diligence. By the 1820s the fashionable family home he built in Edinburgh's New Town was a haven, not only for distinguished visitors and professionals, but for anyone working in the lighthouse service:

No servant of the Northern Lights came to Edinburgh but he was entertained at Baxter's Place to breakfast. There, at his own table, my grandfather sat down delightedly with his broad-spoken, homespun officers. His whole relation to the service was, in fact, patriarchal; and I believe I may say that throughout its ranks he was adored. I have spoken with many who knew him; I was his grandson, and their words may have very well been words of flattery; but there was one thing that could not be affected, and that was the look and light that came into their faces at the name of Robert Stevenson.

Away from Edinburgh, Robert shouldered enormous responsibility for the construction and smooth running of the Scottish lights, often in desolate places completely cut off from civilisation:

Lighthouse operations in Scotland differed essentially in character from those in England. The English coast is in comparison a habitable, homely place, well supplied with towns; the Scottish presents hundreds of miles of savage islands and desolate moors. The Parliamentary committee of 1834, profoundly ignorant of this distinction, insisted with my grandfather that the work at the various stations should be let out on contract 'in the neighbourhood,' where sheep and deer, and gulls and cormorants, and a few ragged gillies, perhaps crouching in a bee-hive house, made up the only neighbours. In such situations repairs and improvements could only be overtaken by collecting (as my grandfather expressed it) a few 'lads,' placing them under charge of a foreman, and despatching them about the coast as occasion served. The particular danger of these seas increased the difficulty.

RLS was clearly in awe of his grandfather's love of dangerous voyages around the coast in the lighthouse vessel, especially as he had found his own experiences in Orkney, Fair Isle, and Shetland aboard *Pharos* so uncongenial:

It must not be forgotten that these voyages in the tender were the particular pleasure and reward of his existence; that he had in him a reserve of romance which carried him delightedly over these hardships and perils; that to him it was 'great gain' to be eight nights and seven days in the savage bay of Levenswick [Shetland] — to read a book in the much agitated cabin — to go on deck and hear the gale scream in his ears, and see the landscape dark with rain and the ship plunge at her two anchors …

The grandson also relates, with near incredulity, a story told him in childhood by his father. Thomas, still just a boy, had been taken by Robert on an annual inspection around the coastlines of Scotland, including Orkney. The well-known perils of the Pentland Firth were bad enough, but on this occasion the lighthouse yacht *Regent* was nearly scuppered by the locals' callous indifference to the fate of mariners:

> On a September night, the *Regent* lay in the Pentland Firth in a fog and a violent and windless swell. It was still dark, when they were alarmed by the sound of breakers, and an anchor was immediately let go. The peep of dawn discovered them swinging in desperate proximity to the Isle of Swona and the surf bursting close under their stern. There was in this place a hamlet of the inhabitants, fisher-folk and wreckers; their huts stood close about the head of the beach. All slept; the doors were closed, and there was no smoke, and the anxious watchers on board ship seemed to contemplate a village of the dead. It was thought possible to launch a boat and tow the *Regent* from her place of danger; and with this view a signal of distress was made and a gun fired with a red-hot poker from the galley. Its detonation awoke the sleepers. Door after door was opened, and in the grey light of the morning fisher after fisher was seen to come forth, yawning and stretching himself, nightcap on head. Fisher after fisher, I wrote, and my pen tripped; for it should rather stand wrecker after wrecker. There was no emotion, no animation, it scarce seemed any interest; not a hand was raised; but all callously awaited the harvest of the sea, and their children stood by their side and waited also. To the end of his life, my father remembered that amphitheatre of placid spectators on the beach; and with a special and natural animosity, the boys of his own age. But presently a light air sprang up, and filled the sails, and fainted, and filled them again; and little by little the *Regent* fetched way against the swell, and clawed off shore into the turbulent firth.

This dreadful incident left a lasting impression on three Stevenson generations and showed only too clearly that 19th-century lighthouse engineering, dedicated to protecting lives at sea, sometimes had to contend with callous ones on land.

Robert Louis Stevenson's artistry has left us a wealth of impressions about the Stevenson engineers who served the Northern Lights. There is no doubt that the errant youth who rebelled against parental expectations finally came to a deep appreciation of the contributions his relatives had made to protecting lives at sea:

> There is scarce a deep sea light from the Isle of Man to North Berwick,
> But one of my blood designed it.
> The Bell Rock stands monument for my grandfather;
> The Skerry Vhor for my uncle Alan;
> And when the lights come out along the shores of Scotland,
> I am proud to think that they burn more brightly for the genius of my father.

The statue of Robert Louis Stevenson in Colinton, Edinburgh (Wikipedia/Sylvia Stanley).

One of the world's best-loved storytellers may have ended up half a world away from his birthplace, but he is still celebrated in Edinburgh – not by the tallest memorial ever raised to a writer, but by an intimate statue of a young wordsmith with his Skye terrier, placed close to the Manse where he spent some of the happiest days of his childhood.

6 DESTINATION MUCKLE FLUGGA

A DAUNTING CHALLENGE

Muckle Flugga and its 'Impossible Lighthouse' (photo: Paul Warrener).

Our travels among the lighthouses of Orkney and Shetland have ranged widely, from the Pentland Skerries to far-flung Muckle Flugga and back again; under our own steam as well as in the 19th-century company of an enthusiastic Walter Scott and a deeply troubled Robert Louis Stevenson; in moods as fickle as the wild northern seas. And now, as a final comment on the brilliance of the Stevenson lighthouse pioneers, we return to one of their most iconic creations, a daunting challenge against enormous odds.

In February 1854 David Stevenson, recently appointed Engineer to the Northern Lighthouse Board in place of his brother Alan, sailed to the far north of Shetland to explore locations for new lighthouses. He was under extreme pressure. The Crimean War had broken out the year before and the British navy was tasked with blockading the Russian port of Archangel in the White Sea, high above the Arctic Circle, to stop Tsar Nicholas's warships reaching the Mediterranean.

The navy's North Sea Squadron had to negotiate its way past the Orkney and Shetland Islands, avoid calamity along Norway's 1,000-mile coastline, and skirt around the North Cape. And it had better return safely. The Admiralty, still bruised by the wreck of two warships on the coast of Jutland in 1811 with the loss of 1,421 lives, was nervous of northern waters. Backed by the British government, it demanded two new lights on the treacherous northeast coastlines of Shetland – and by October of the same year 'if possible'.

When David had first sailed to Shetland with his father at the tender age of 13 his spirit and stomach survived North Sea storms unscathed; but this time, at the ripe old age of 39, conditions were less to his liking:

> The weather was wretched and the passage most uncomfortable and on arriving at Lerwick on Saturday night at 11 oclock, having experienced considerable difficulty in finding the entrance to the Bay, we were informed that the last mail received at Shetland was on 1st December 1853 and that the winter had been an unusually severe one … our appearance off the coast at that season of the year caused no small speculation among the simple islanders. The rumour of the war too it seems had reached them … they all retreated to the interior leaving their houses to our mercy and we learned afterwards that they were afraid of the press gang or that we might be Russians.

Continuing northwards from Lerwick, David investigated several possible lighthouse sites: Out Skerries near the island of Whalsay, about 30 miles north of Lerwick; Baltasound and Lamba Ness on Unst, Shetland's furthest island; and the awesome rock of Muckle Flugga, a mile or so beyond the tip of Unst. Appalling weather prevented him from landing but he got sufficiently close to conclude that it was 'not practicable to erect and maintain a lighthouse upon these rocks'. He reported that conditions around Shetland's north and east coastlines made lighthouse building 'impossible, impractical, dangerous, too expensive, and any ship that took that route was mad anyway'. It was far better to pass from the North Sea to the Atlantic between Orkney and Shetland, a course already made safer by his father's lighthouse on Sumburgh Head and Alan's fine new one on North Ronaldsay, lit the year before.

Unfortunately for the Commissioners of the Northern Lighthouse Board and their new Engineer, the Lords of the Admiralty were adamant. In those days the government department responsible for British lighthouses was the Board of Trade. Trinity House, which built and maintained the English lights, also had considerable authority over the Northern Lighthouse Board. So any negotiations between Edinburgh and London involved an elaborate chain of command and, more often than not, a lot of wrangling.

The Commissioners warned the Board of Trade that 'it would be culpable recklessness as regards the lives of the lightkeepers to erect even a temporary lighthouse on the Flugga'. Unconvinced, the Board sent a party of Elder Brethren of Trinity House to Unst in June 1854 to inspect the site for themselves. They made an easy landing on Muckle Flugga from an unusually placid sea and decided that the Commissioners were making a fuss – it would be quite possible for their 'eminent engineer' to build a lighthouse on the summit.

Needless to say, London got its way. Although David's proposed light on Out Skerries was accepted, a second one at Lamba Ness on Unst was refused. The Admiralty's top

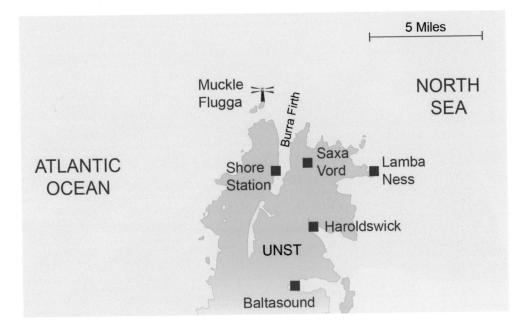

The northern part of Unst, showing Muckle Flugga and its shore station.

priority remained Muckle Flugga, not so much for ships sailing to the White Sea as for those returning home. Shetland's northernmost rocks lay in wait, surrounded by some of the severest weather in the world, and London valued the safety of the Royal Navy above the comfort of Scottish lighthouse engineers.

A few months later Thomas Stevenson and Alan Brebner, son of a mason who had worked on the Bell Rock Lighthouse and by now one of the Stevensons' most trusted resident engineers, visited Unst and clambered onto Muckle Flugga. A hair-raising scramble to the top confirmed that there was just about enough space for a temporary light or beacon.

The turn of events must have been hard for David, in constant demand as an international authority on docks, harbours, and river engineering as well as general manager of the family firm in Edinburgh. He had watched Alan succumb to a progressive illness, aggravated by severe overwork, and had tried, but failed, to persuade the Northern Lighthouse Board to share his own appointment with Thomas. He was now being landed with an extreme form of lighthouse engineering and had few illusions, describing Muckle Flugga as:

> an outlying rock of a conical form, called a "stack", which rises to the height of nearly 200 feet above the sea. Towards the north its face is nearly perpendicular, and exposed to the full "fetch" of the Northern Ocean. Its southern face is a steep rocky slope, which, previous to the cutting of steps on its surface, could only be scaled with great difficulty ... There is only one part of the rock at which a landing can be effected, and that of course only in favourable weather.

Muckle Flugga from the south, with Out Stack beyond (Geograph/Andy Strangeway).

Muckle Flugga and the neighbouring stacks of Tipta, Rumblings, and Vesta Skerry (Geograph/Mike Pennington).

Actually Muckle Flugga ('large steep-sided island' in Old Norse) is not quite the last outpost of the British Isles – a distinction that belongs to Out Stack, a smaller and much lower rock about half a mile further north. Nor is Muckle Flugga entirely isolated; neighbouring stacks including Tipta, Rumblings and Vesta Skerry continue for a mile southwards. But as far as a lighthouse site was concerned, Muckle Flugga was the best of a bad lot.

On his return to Edinburgh from Shetland, David had no alternative but to bite the bullet. He immediately set about designing wooden towers to support two temporary lights, and iron barracks for the keepers. Vessels were hired to ship all components, materials, tools, and provisions to the far north. The intense pressure made him feel very much alone and 'by no means well' as he and his assistants struggled valiantly to meet the Admiralty's deadlines.

The light on Out Skerries near Whalsay was completed by mid-September, but Muckle Flugga took a few weeks longer:

> The first light on this rock was shown from a temporary tower, erected in 1854, at the suggestion of the Admiralty, for the benefit of the North Sea Squadron, then engaged in prosecuting the Russian war. The Government deemed it advisable to provide certain lights before winter set in, and only a few months remained to make all the necessary preparations for indicating to our navy the rugged shores of Northern Shetland. The "Pharos" steamer left Glasgow, with the workmen and temporary lighthouse and dwellings, on the 31st July, and the light was exhibited on the 11th October; and when it is considered that the whole of the materials and stores (consisting of water, cement, lime, coal, iron-work, glass, and provisions, and weighing upwards of 120 tons) had to be landed on an exposed rock, and carried up to the top in small quantities on the backs of labourers, it will be seen that the exertions of Mr. Brebner, who acted as resident engineer, and of Mr. Watt, who took charge of the landing department, were in the highest degree praiseworthy.

It was a remarkable achievement, accomplished in 'the wonderfully short space of twenty six days' by 20 masons housed on the rock, assisted by local labourers who made a daily crossing from a shore base in Burra Firth. If we take a 19th-century 'small quantity' as 50 pounds, the 120 tons of materials and stores must have needed around 5,000 individual journeys up and down the treacherous eastern rock face on rough-hewn steps, steadied by lifelines attached to the summit. The installation was protected by a dyke of rubble quarried on the rock itself, set in cement. No wonder David acknowledged the efforts of Messrs Brebner and Watt.

Unfortunately inauguration of Muckle Flugga's temporary light by no means signalled the end of their woes. Everyone had assumed that a site 200 feet above the surrounding ocean, battered by storm-force winds, would at least be spared the attention of storm-force

Modern ladders to the top: some of the original rough-hewn stone steps can also be detected in this photograph of Muckle Flugga's eastern rock face (Wikipedia/Smith609).

waves. But the foreman of the quarriers, Mr Charles Barclay, who was left to complete the cutting of steps in the rock face, reported that on 3 December:

> the sea began to break over the rock about 9 A.M., and increased in weight until 1 o'clock: several seas thereafter broke heavily on the tower, and one of them burst open the door of the dwelling-house, deluging the whole with water … The sea was all like smoke as far as we could see and the noise which the wind made on the roof of our House and on the tower was like thunder … the water came pouring in upon us, so that we had to drive it out (as much as possible) with a mop and brush &c before the next spray came.

The storms continued, carrying away huge fresh water casks and large sections of the protective dyke, destroying the coal house, and terrifying the men who 'had not a dry part to sit down in or even a dry bed to rest upon at night'. Sea water broke against the tower and ran up the side, damaging the lantern. By the end of December the men were exhausted and demoralised, so much so that David, fearing for their safety, reported to the Board of Trade that 'life is in jeopardy'. This time London was more understanding and, although refusing evacuation of the temporary light during the winter months, agreed to replace it with something far more robust.

Needless to say the Board of Trade wanted the permanent replacement on Muckle Flugga, whereas the Northern Lighthouse Board still favoured Lamba Ness, David's original suggestion, a far easier location. After further tetchy bargaining London prevailed, and orders to proceed were given in June 1855, with construction scheduled for 1856. In the meantime David finally convinced the Board that his appointment could be shared with Thomas, making the brothers jointly responsible for tackling one of the greatest challenges ever faced by the Stevenson engineers. The lighthouse – as mentioned earlier, initially known as North Unst – would be completed two years after the Crimean War ended. By a strange irony Florence Nightingale and the Charge of the Light Brigade entered British military history, but the Royal Navy's heroic blockade of the White Sea was largely forgotten.

We now digress a little to talk about Unst, base for all the Muckle Flugga operations. A fascinating island of 60 square miles with a current population of about 700, it now boasts a heritage centre, a museum dedicated to its unique wooden boats and the fishermen who sailed them, a proud tradition of breeding Shetland ponies, two nature reserves of national significance, and some wonderful sandy beaches. It is also a birdwatcher's paradise. More than 100,000 seabirds including gannets, puffins, fulmars, guillemots, razorbills, and kittiwakes crowd its stunning sea cliffs in the breeding season; and it is one of the last strongholds of the great skua, or 'bonxie', the flying pirate that bullies other birds into surrendering their latest meal. The Hermaness national nature reserve in the northwest of the island has a car park and visitor centre at Muckle Flugga's former shore station. This makes it a good place to observe the bonxie's tactics – and to spy Shetland's remarkable lighthouse.

Most visitors reach Unst by the 10-minute ferry crossing from neighbouring Yell and dock at Belmont in the far southwest of the island. Shortly after leaving Belmont you can make

Gannets on Unst, with Muckle Flugga in the background (Geograph/Mike Pennington).

an interesting detour to the desolate but impressive ruins of Muness Castle, built in 1598, before continuing north to the island's main settlement of Baltasound, a former capital of the herring industry that reached seasonal populations of thousands in its heyday. Nowadays Baltasound boasts what is claimed to be the world's most famous bus shelter. Three miles further on is little Haroldswick, which for many years hosted the United Kingdom's most northerly post office. The famous red building appeared on a 20p stamp in 1997, two years before its closure because there was nobody to take over from the retiring postmistress; but the settlement still includes Britain's most northerly church.

Vernacular buildings of Unst: the famous bus shelter at Baltasound (Wikipedia); the former post office at Haroldswick (Wikipedia); and Haroldswick Methodist Church (Geograph/Mike Pennington).

The former lighthouse shore station on Burra Firth, with Saxa Vord in the background (Geograph/Mike Pennington).

Looking towards Muckle Flugga from Saxa Vord. The rock on the right is Out Stack, final northern outpost of the British Isles (Geograph/Mike Pennington).

Finally, you come to the furthest reaches of the British Isles. The views from Saxa Vord, Unst's highest hill, are spectacular. An unofficial UK wind speed record of 177mph was recorded here in 1962. Far below, the long sea loch of Burra Firth provides a sheltered anchorage for the former shore station; and a mile off shore to the northwest, the building that has enticed us all the way from John o' Groats stands defiant on its stack.

David and Thomas Stevenson were very different characters. As we have seen, David was cut out from the start to be a professional engineer, and followed his father into the family business as naturally as a duck takes to water. More a manager than an adventurer, he was internationally recognised as an expert on harbours, docks, and river engineering. Thomas entered the family business more by accident than design and, although ending up as a world expert on lighthouse illumination, remained a romantic at heart, less interested in business and project management than research and development.

The brothers seem an unlikely pair of professional colleagues, yet they held their joint appointment with the Northern Lighthouse Board for 26 years, a remarkable period in which they designed and built 25 Scottish lighthouses. Abroad, the firm's consulting activities included lighting the coastlines of New Zealand and Japan. A lot of give-and-take must have been required in their working relationship, yet they seem to have managed it well, understanding and accepting one another's strengths and weaknesses.

Their joint appointment had only just started when the call came loud and clear from London for a permanent lighthouse on Muckle Flugga. Although David had designed the temporary light he was tied up once again with other civil engineering projects. Thomas had some fairly recent lighthouse experience of a gentler kind, including construction of the Little Ross Light near Kirkcudbright. But neither brother had designed a permanent rock lighthouse remotely comparable to their father's Bell Rock or Alan's Skerryvore. Muckle Flugga had to perch on a dramatic clifftop, not a reef at sea level. David undertook much of the initial design work, but as construction got under way Thomas accepted increasing responsibility, and today the Northern Lighthouse Board credits Thomas and David Stevenson – in that order – as joint Engineers of one of its most famous creations.

The western face of Muckle Flugga (photo: Paul Warrener).

A major decision concerned material for the tower. Bell Rock and Skerryvore were both constructed using massive stone blocks, fashioned by skilled masons to demanding tolerances and fitted together like gigantic jigsaw puzzles. But blocks weighing a ton or more were out of the question for Muckle Flugga. It would be difficult if not impossible to land them, let alone haul them to the top.

The solution was bricks. Alan Stevenson had used them for his recently completed North Ronaldsay Lighthouse because there was no suitable local stone. But his building was not under constant attack by violent salt water and the brothers were acutely aware that a brick tower on Muckle Flugga would represent a radical departure, 'an untried experiment in marine engineering'. The obvious advantage was that bricks could be transported in open boats and landed, if necessary, by throwing them to colleagues standing at the base of the near-vertical cliff face. But a huge number would be needed.

The earth's curvature makes the range of a lighthouse highly dependent on its elevation above sea level. Wave-washed Bell Rock achieved a range of about 15 miles with a 100-foot tower; Skerryvore, built a few feet above sea level, managed 18 miles with 138 feet. Muckle Flugga, on top of a 200-foot stack, would obviously start with a big height advantage – indeed a low, squat, tower would have been quite adequate from the range point of view. But there was another vital consideration: David's temporary light, atop a 21-foot tower, had proved extremely vulnerable to violent seawater, so more height was clearly essential. It was a classic design decision – build higher and safer, or lower and cheaper? Carefully weighing the evidence obtained since February 1854, he opted for a 64-foot tower.

David's conical tower had to survive assault by hurricane-force winds as well as sea water, and needed exceptional foundations. His design specified brick walls tapering from

Arrival at the summit, and the 64-foot brick tower (Geograph/Mike Pennington).

three and a half feet thick at the top to four and a half at the base, sunk 10 feet into solid rock. Unreliable local stone was unacceptable, even for rubble infill. A simple, unfussy, cornice topped the walls, with iron instead of the usual stone for the internal floors and light-room pedestal. A 5-foot protective wall around the building would help subdue wave impacts and provide some protection for men moving around outside.

It was clear that raising bricks and other materials to the summit of Muckle Flugga would be a huge undertaking. David decided that steam power, the great enabling technology of the 19th century, must be pressed into service. An inclined plane operated by a 10 HP steam engine, similar in principle to those used for many years on the English canal system, could save time and the back-breaking labour of about 20 men.

Work began in April 1856 and in just over a month the steam engine, boiler, and iron components for a workmen's barrack were somehow manhandled to the summit and installed. The work was so dangerous and uncongenial that the men had to be paid half-a-crown a day, double the going rate on Unst. Workshops and accommodation were started at Burra Firth, and more than 100 men joined the workforce as the season developed. It took about 18 months to complete the building works on the rock, often in appalling weather. On many occasions sea water reached the summit and swirled around the men's feet; in extreme wind conditions they had to crawl around on hands and knees. But in spite of all the trials and tribulations the permanent light was commissioned on 1 January 1858.

Over the intervening years there have been many reports of storm damage to the protective wall, waves propelling heavy items across the courtyard, keepers stranded for weeks beyond their expected term of duty, and boatmen taking risks to rescue them. Lantern panes have been broken. On one occasion a live fish was found in a pool on the summit. A posting to Muckle Flugga became regarded as one of the most demanding in the Scottish lighthouse service, only suitable for its most resilient employees who, perhaps unsurprisingly, referred to it as 'the Flugga'. Yet throughout more than a century and a half, the lighthouse tower and associated buildings have stayed resolutely firm and – despite the brick construction – impressively waterproof.

A team of six keepers kept the light burning for up to 18 hours in the long nights of a Shetland winter. Three were on duty for a month at a time, while the others waited their turn in the shore station on Burra Firth. It was the Northern Lighthouse Board's policy to have three keepers rather than two on duty in its remote rock lighthouses in case one became sick or was injured. It was also rumoured that, in the case of a death, two survivors could provide a more convincing assurance that no foul play had occurred.

The Board was fully aware of the special strengths required of its keepers:

> Not everyone is suitable to be a light keeper. The good light keeper has, or acquires, the temperament necessary for the job, which involves residence close to the sea and has much loneliness and isolation in its composition. The primary duty is to keep watch at night, to ensure that his light flashes correctly to character ... a light keeper must be a man of parts ... a handyman of varying

A glimpse of Muckle Flugga from the north of Unst; landing stores at the base of the rock (Geograph/Mike Pennington).

proficiency but mostly of a high standard … a useful cook and a good companion. A light keeper will not make a fortune but he will be at peace with himself and the world.

Muckle Flugga's supply boat was the vital point of contact with keepers on the rock, and its skipper took responsibility for the safe delivery of personnel, equipment and supplies from the shore station. Initially everything including drinking water and fuel for the light was transported by boat, landed at the base of the cliff, and hauled to the top by the rail and bogie system (inclined plane). Later a Blondin aerial ropeway was installed, allowing goods to be hoisted straight off the boat to the summit. An expert judge of wind, wave, and tide, the boatman had to decide whether a landing was feasible. He and his crew were mainly local men who served for many years, unlike the keepers who were posted from one lighthouse to another.

The shore station, an impressive Victorian building, provided generous accommodation for keepers and their families, plus boatshed, workshop, storage facilities, slipway, and derrick. In the early days communication with the rock was by semaphore signalling from the top of Hermaness Hill, but radio was installed in 1939. This offered wives a chance to chat with their husbands offshore – but unfortunately not in privacy because some of the Unst locals were expert eavesdroppers. Today the shore station houses a visitor centre for the Hermaness Nature Reserve.

For just over a century the lighthouse kept its rather prosaic name of North Unst. It was in 1964 that this was changed to Muckle Flugga, far more expressive and, to all but Gaelic speakers, wonderfully suggestive. The fixed light was changed to flashing in 1928, with a range of about 25 miles. In the late 1960s the keepers' notoriously cramped accommodation – they 'slept in a crow's nest and ate in a cell' – was upgraded, and electricity installed. Nowadays a helipad provides access that would have been unimaginable to the generations who struggled from Burra Firth in small boats, squeezed into the narrow gully below the eastern cliff face, and scaled the dizzy heights on aching limbs.

Lights in the North (Geograph/Mike Pennington).

Automation came to Muckle Flugga in 1995 and the lighthouse said farewell to its keepers. But one of Scotland's most historic lights remains in service, piercing the northern darkness night after night, a welcome assurance to sailors that they are where they think they are, a warning in moments of doubt, a signal service rendered *in salutem omnium*.

INDEX

Note: figures in bold type indicate an illustration.